The Handmaid's Tale

MARGARET ATWOOD

Guide written by

Sandra Langdon

A *Letts* EXPLORE **Literature Guide**

First published 1998

Letts Educational
Aldine House
Aldine Place
London W12 8AW
0181 740 2266

Text © Sandra Langdon

Series editor Ron Simpson

Typeset by Jordan Publishing Design

Text design Jonathan Barnard

Cover and text illustrations Ivan Allen

Design © BPP (Letts Educational) Ltd

Acknowledgements

Extracts from *The Handmaid's Tale* by Margaret Atwood are reproduced by kind permission of the publisher, Jonathan Cape.

British Library Cataloguing in Publication Data
A CIP record for this book is available from the British Library

ISBN 1 85758 843 6

Printed and bound in Great Britain

Ashford Colour Press, Gosport, Hampshire

Letts Educational is the trading name of BPP (Letts Educational) Ltd

■ Contents

◼ Plot synopsis

The Handmaid's Tale is a transcribed account of one Handmaid's third posting in the early twentieth-century Republic of Gilead, formerly the United States of America. The Republic is a patriarchal regime, founded on a fundamentalist Christian response to declining Caucasian birth rates in the permissive generations of the late twentieth century. The government rules through force, oppression and state controlled technology. Biblical teachings are distorted as a means of control and to justify inhumane state practices. All forms of communication have been banned. Women are categorised according to age, marital status and reproductive ability. Men are categorised according to age and membership as Commanders of the Faith in the elite Sons of Jacob. Older single women, gay men and barren Handmaids are sent to the Colonies to clean up after warfare and toxic spills. A Handmaid serves as a surrogate mother for the childless wives of Commanders.

The story is set in Cambridge, Massachusetts. The narrative opens with Offred, lying in her bed, recalling the Red Centre where she trained to become a Handmaid. The next day she does the daily household shopping with her partner, Ofglen. Each time they go shopping Offred and Ofglen visit the Wall where the bodies of executed dissenters are hung. Both women check the Wall for the bodies of loved ones. At night Offred travels through her memory as a form of resistance against accepting her Gileadean existence. At these times she thinks of her husband, daughter, mother and her college friend Moira during the time before the Republic.

While they are shopping, Offred is unaware that Ofglen uses the resistance movement password in conversation with her. In her room she recalls how she came across a message in her cupboard from her predecessor. The message becomes a talisman of Offred's resistance to the system. The previous day, during her monthly check-up, the doctor had offered to impregnate Offred because her time as a Handmaid is running out – if she does not become pregnant soon she will be considered barren and sent to the colonies. Afraid of the consequences if someone were to find out that she had become pregnant by the doctor, she declined his offer.

While she has her bath Offred thinks of her daughter. She takes a nap and as she dozes she recalls Moira's arrival at the Red Centre, she dreams that Luke, her husband, is dead and she dreams of her failed escape with her daughter. It is evening of the monthly fertilisation Ceremony with the Commander and his wife based on the Book of Genesis. In the sitting room before the prayers,

Nick, the Commander's personal assistant, touches Offred's foot. The television news is on while they wait for the Commander's arrival, and she hears the state propaganda about the wars Gilead is fighting and the repatriation programme for black Americans. She recalls more details of her failed escape. Offred is unable to pray because of the regime's inhumanity to women. She remembers Moira's torture after a bungled escape attempt from the Red Centre. Restless after the Ceremony, she steals a daffodil from the sitting room and is startled by Nick. They indulge in a passionate embrace. He informs her that the Commander wishes to start seeing her privately in his office. In bed, she feels guilty for desiring Nick and wonders what happened to Luke. The following day she attends the Birth Day of a Handmaid, Janine, from the Centre. This is strictly a women's event, and Offred thinks of her mother, a feminist, who wanted a women's culture. Exhausted after the proceedings, she tells the reader the story of Moira's successful escape from the Red Centre. That evening she meets with the Commander and they play Scrabble. When she returns to her room she laughs herself asleep in her cupboard.

As May passes into June, Offred's becomes the Commander's mistress. During these meetings she is allowed forbidden items such as books and moisturising cream. Ofglen tells Offred about the Mayday resistance movement. During her nap on this day she recollects the beginning of the take over by the Sons of Jacob. At her clandestine meeting with the Commander he tells her that the previous Offred hanged herself. She fears that her memories of Luke and her daughter are fading. The following day Serena Joy, the Commander's Wife, offers to arrange for Offred to sleep with Nick in order to improve her chances of conceiving. As payment for agreeing, Serena Joy will procure a photo of Offred's daughter for her.

Offred attends a Prayvaganza, which is a mass wedding between Guardians and Daughters. Ofglen tells her that Janine's baby was declared an Unbaby and destroyed. Offred is deeply upset that love is no longer valued within the regime. Her will to survive is dealt a severe blow when she sees the recent photograph of her daughter, because she knows that she has probably forgotten her biological mother.

That evening the Commander smuggles Offred out to the state brothel, housed in the hotel where she used to enjoy illicit meetings with Luke. Here she is reunited with Moira. Moira tells Offred of the Underground Femaleroad to Canada, of life in the Colonies and of what the regime did to Offred's mother. Offred is disappointed that Moira has resigned herself to the life of a prostitute. At the hotel the Commander feebly tries to have intercourse with Offred, who secretly finds him repellent. Later that night she enjoys her arranged meeting with Nick.

Having fallen in love with Nick, Offred no longer desires to escape from Gilead. She attends a Women's Salvaging (execution) followed by a

Particicution. Before the other Handmaids can tear the man apart, Ofglen kicks him unconscious because he is a member of the resistance, not a rapist as the regime claims. Janine has a nervous breakdown following her part in the man's murder. That afternoon Ofglen is replaced by a new Handmaid, who informs Offred that Ofglen hanged herself because the black van was coming for her. When Offred gets home, Serena Joy accuses her of betrayal, having evidence of her visit to Jezebel's, the brothel. In her room she hears the black van coming for her. Nick arrives and tells her it is really Mayday. He reassures her by using her real name. Her story ends with her assent into the van, not knowing whether she is being rescued or arrested.

Almost two hundred years later, Offred's narrative is the subject of a conference on Gileadean Studies held in the Arctic. The keynote speaker, in trying to authenticate Offred's story, misses its significance as a feminine account of life in a patriarchal society.

■ Who's who in *The Handmaid's Tale*

Offred

Offred

The narrator's real name is never revealed, unless it is June, the only Handmaid's name exchanged between beds at the Red Centre not associated with a specific character. She identifies herself as Offred, a patronymic, derived from the possessive preposition and her Commander's first name.

As the protagonist and narrator, she is the most fully realised character. She tells her story of being stripped of her freedom and forced to live under a bizarre patriarchal system where women are debased as reproductive symbols. She survives by silently rebelling against the system. Her ironic, and at times cynical, sense of humour and memories of her former identities as mother, wife, lover, daughter and career woman protect her from psychologically adopting the role of Handmaid assigned her.

Bored, lonely, sexually and intellectually frustrated, she manages to separate her body from her mind. She is also adept at finding ways to make her incredibly restricted life more interesting. She plays word games with herself and ·enjoys the secret subversive life of Serena Joy's garden. Her observations of the people who inhabit her story and the world around her are astute, satirical, detailed and precise.

She is a self-conscious narrator, deeply aware of the significance and flaws of the act of storytelling. She is human, and is at various times cowardly, confused, selfish and emotional. Her integrity forces her to recount painful events and undesirable feelings in order to communicate the truth of her experiences. She also retains her privacy, in not sharing her real name, her daughter's name or details of her first night with Nick.

Independent and feminine, she presents a middle ground between the extremes of feminism (her mother and Moira) and servility (Janine). Educated, intelligent and sensible, she sees the ironies and contradictions of both the time before and the Gileadean regime. Although many of her choices are limited, she takes responsibility for her actions. She is aware of her betrayals of Luke and the Commander's household. She also comes to regret her earlier embarrassment of her mother. Her will to survive is fuelled by her belief in love: romantic, sexual and charitable.

Her life in the time before was characterised by the simple pleasures of motherhood, marriage, meaningful work and friendship. Unlike her mother and Moira, she was not political and enjoyed the traditional domestic arrangement of the family. She did not foresee the downfall of democratic America. We do not know what happened to her after the end of her narrative.

The Commander

In her description of his entrance to the household prayers, Offred describes the Commander in a panorama of changing images. This description is fitting, as our impression of the Commander is constantly changing. Despite his relationship with Offred being the most vividly portrayed in the narrative, he remains an elusive character. Professionally he is a ruthless and imposing figure. Well educated and deceptively clever, he is among the elite responsible for the take over and implementation of policy. Although able to justify each of his harsh stances, he is blind to their emotional consequences. For instance, he fails to see that it is equally debasing to women for them to be regarded as wombs, as it is for them to be valued as sex objects. He also has little idea of the restricted nature of a Handmaid's existence.

In their personal relationship, Offred describes him as 'positively daddyish'. Lonely and isolated within the regime, he breaks his own rules in his need for human contact and sexual variety. As the novel progresses, he becomes increasingly unlikeable. Whilst his attitude towards Offred is endearingly paternal, it is also patronising, owing to the inherent imbalance of power between parents and children. His ignorance, opinions and behaviour at Jezebel's are deeply sexist. As he watches the Eyes escort Offred to the black van, he is portrayed as an ageing vulnerable old man. The *Historical Notes* suggest he was executed shortly thereafter in an early purge of liberal tendencies among the elite. Through his arrogance and weakness, which cause his downfall, he gives the regime a human face.

Serena Joy

Serena Joy represents the spurned wife. Although she resents the procreation arrangements, she is desperate to have a child through Offred, having been cruelly denied the opportunity by nature. She indulges her mothering aspirations in her garden and her knitting. A former television evangelist who advocated that a woman's place is in the home, she finds herself trapped in her own ideals. Her frustration and unhappiness are evident in her chain smoking and surly manner. Contrary to what she preached, she is happiest outside the home or reminiscing about her singing career. Her real name is Pam.

She is an acrimonious figure: jealous, gossiping, cold and vindictive. During the Ceremony she purposely makes Offred as uncomfortable as possible. She is, nevertheless, the most important female figure in Offred's daily life. Like Offred, she believes in love. She and her husband may inhabit different areas of the house and spend little time together, but Serena Joy's love for him is manifest in her possessiveness and outrage upon discovering the purple sequinned costume and telltale lipstick on her cloak.

Serena Joy is both wretched and generous to Offred. She obviously knew the whereabouts of Offred's daughter before she offered to obtain the photograph. She is, however, also responsible for Offred's brief period of happiness and fulfilment under the regime. It was Serena Joy who organised the first meeting with Nick. It was not Serena Joy who ordered the black van for Offred. Infuriated as she was on uncovering Offred's affair with her husband, she feels more betrayed at the Handmaid's sudden departure for 'Violation of state secrets'. It is likely that Offred's departure brought about the demise of the household, and the Commander's death. Serena Joy's position within Gilead was never secure, hence her pretensions of piety: the soul scrolls and painting of alleged Puritan ancestors. Serena Joy is not as wicked, or as fearsome, as the Aunts are. She arouses our pity.

Nick

A mysterious character, Nick is attractive and sexy. Being a member of the Eyes, his casual manner is understandable. At the same time, he is a trusted member of the household. Outwardly affable, we never know what he is thinking. He displays his own rebellious streak early when he winks at Offred. The ending of Offred's tale invites a possible rereading of Nick's behaviour. Perhaps the naughty wink and touch on her foot at the Prayers were really cryptic messages to her to let her know that he would save her. Nick fulfils Offred's fantasy of being rescued. The message he gives her is her real name before strangers escort her into the black van.

Moira

Moira is the most animated character in the story and a significant influence on Offred. Flamboyantly unconventional, she possesses unshakeable self-assurance. She avoids subscribing to any ideology through her cynical and subversive attitude, both in the time before and in Gileadean society. Her seditious humour at the Red Centre is important to the other Handmaids because it is the only weapon they have against the Aunts' tyranny.

Moira is a lesbian and, like Offred's mother, is a politically aware feminist. She is very conscious of her rights. Unlike Offred's mother, she did not have to fight for equality. Despite her boldness, she is captured and condemned to factious life within the regime.

Luke

Luke represents the 'new man' of the late twentieth century: he is fully involved in child rearing, cooks and is supportive of Offred when she loses her job. He is also intelligent and courageous. His memory is vital to Offred's survival. In terms of characterisation he is presented as a shadowy figure, implying that he is probably dead by the time Offred records her story. Out of all the 'missing persons' in the novel, he is the only one that never resurfaces in Gilead.

The Commander and Nick each emerge as counterparts to Luke in their relationships with Offred. Like the Commander, Luke's relationship with Offred began as an extra-marital affair. They share a love of wordplay which each indulges with Offred. Nick becomes Luke's Gileadean counterpart in Offred's affections. Their names even sound similar.

Offred's mother

Offred's mother was a member of the Women's Liberation movement in the late 1960s and early 1970s. Her participation in demonstrations is based on real events, such as anti-porn book burnings and pro-abortion marches. Like Moira, she is happy to erase men from her life. She never tells Offred who her father is, preferring to bring her daughter up as a single parent in a women-dominated environment.

She is a curious mix of radicalism and tradition. She was a single parent in a time of disapproving attitudes on the part of both the establishment and hard-core feminists. In spite of this, she wanted to experience the traditional rite of passage of motherhood. She refuses to dye her hair, yet preserves her youthful energy by working out at the gym. The sacrifices she made for her bohemian lifestyle are evident. As an older woman she is lonely and disappointed that Offred takes for granted the advances in women's rights that her generation achieved.

A curious parallel can be drawn between Offred's mother and Serena Joy. Though opposites in ideology, each woman is undermined by her ideals under the new regime. Offred's mother is declared an Unwoman due to her age, unmarried status and pro-abortion stance. Tragically for someone who always looked after her health, she is sent to the Colonies to clean up toxic waste. Her life in the time before and after the take over becomes a legacy, though not in the way she had anticipated. Instead of being absolved by history, she lives on in films as an example of the 'Unwomen' who brought about the downfall of society.

Offred's daughter

Offred's daughter remains unnamed to protect her identity in case Offred's tapes were confiscated by the regime. She is separated from Offred when she is five, to grow up as a Commander's daughter. The references to her different ages, during the failed escape and the recent photograph Serena Joy procures, help fix the time between the take-over and Offred's current posting.

Offred's daughter also has a symbolic importance. Offred's loving relationship with her daughter is contrasted by the surrogate role of the Handmaids. If Offred had a baby during one of her postings, she would have been robbed of the opportunity to bond with her child and develop a loving relationship. This idea is poignantly illustrated in Chapter 21, when Janine's baby is given immediately to the Commander's Wife and Janine is pushed out of the way by the burgeoning circle of jubilant Wives.

Offred's identity as a mother is one of many identities stripped from her in Gilead. Compare Offred's relationship with her daughter to Offred's relationship with her mother.

Ofglen

Ofglen is an altruistic heroine. She works tirelessly for the resistance movement, mercifully kicks the innocent man unconscious at the Particicution and bravely kills herself in order to protect others. She serves as a double in different spectrums to both Moira and Offred. Ofglen represents collective resistance in contrast to Moira's lone rebellion. Offred's struggles with cowardice and near conformity, in the face of anticipated torture and harm to others, are offset against Ofglen's decisive courage. The two Handmaids face the same situation of knowing the black van is coming for them, but react differently. Ofglen commits suicide in an act of valour, similar to soldiers who kill themselves rather than being taken prisoner. Offred, instead, remains calm and resigned to her fate. We assume from the Historical Notes that Offred was rescued. Decide for yourself which quality is more desirable in dire situations, Offred's hope and faith that she would be rescued, or Ofglen's courage.

Janine

Janine is a victim of both freedom and oppression. In the time before when women were not protected, she was gang raped. As a Handmaid her deformed baby is declared an Unbaby and destroyed. Rape is a crime of power. There are similarities between the two events. In both situations she is a powerless individual, victimised as a woman, by a powerful group of men. In each case her baby was destroyed. She descends into madness as a result of her part in the Particicution. A devout believer in the system, she is destroyed by its practices. Janine's fragility reinforces Offred's inner strength. As Aunt Lydia's favourite recruit, her character serves as a means of conveying the details of Moira's escape to the other Handmaids.

Other characters within the regime

Aunts are older single women who train Handmaids, deliver babies and preside over Salvagings. The most abhorrent is Aunt Lydia.

Angels is the name given to the soldiers of the Gileadean army.

Marthas are female servants such as cooks and housekeepers.

Guardians of the Faith are the members of the police force.

The Eyes are the secret police within the Guardians.

Econowives are the wives of common men.

Themes, images and language in *The Handmaid's Tale*

Dystopian literature

Dystopian literature

The Handmaid's Tale can be categorised into several literary genres. A futuristic society is presented. Novels that present dysfunctional futuristic societies are categorised as anti-utopian or dystopian. *The Handmaid's Tale* is a satire of a futuristic world in the tradition of dystopian literature. A dystopia is an imaginary society characterised by inequality and a lack of freedom. Other well-known dystopian novels are Aldous Huxley's *Brave New World* and George Orwell's *Nineteen Eighty-four*.

The Handmaid's Tale shares many features with *Nineteen Eighty-four*. Both novels tell the story of a near-future oppressive society governed by an elite and characterised by distorted language. The societies in each novel are at war, block external influences, use propaganda to further the ideology of the society, rule by force and severely restrict individual freedom. Each novel presents extreme realisations of current societal trends. An author's purpose in writing dystopian novels is to explore the possible development of current societal trends and warn readers of their potentially dangerous consequences.

Margaret Atwood collected newspaper clippings reporting events and developments within the feminist movement, religious right-wing groups in America, and various cultural practices around the world. The clippings revealed emerging trends, and Atwood integrated and worked these ideas through to an extreme conclusion, resulting in the Republic of Gilead. Satire is a form of writing in which societal practices are ridiculed to expose vice or folly. Which current trends are satirised in the novel?

Women and feminism

Women and feminism

Feminism is a difficult word to define. Originally the term referred to equal rights for women. The first wave of feminism began in the nineteenth century and was concerned with the sexual division of labour. The second wave of feminism started in the 1960s, and was originally known as the Women's Liberation Movement. This second wave of feminism is concerned with liberation from male subordination through language and culture. It seeks to create a woman-centred world-view. It has developed many branches: by the 1980s, some branches within the feminist movement started going beyond desiring equal rights with men, to wanting superiority over men. Many women felt criticised by some feminists for wanting to at stay home with their children. Offred's Mother was a member of the Women's Liberation Movement, and she felt criticised by some of her friends for having Offred. Such directions inevitably caused a backlash amongst both men and women. Many felt that extremism within the movement was setting women back culturally.

In the novel, Atwood extrapolates from militant feminist ideas such as the desire for freedom from pornography and freedom from sexual violence. The novel challenges us to consider at what cost we are willing to achieve absolute freedom from these things. Atwood also creates a women's culture. In Gilead women are categorised according to their age, marital status and fertility. Women are controlled by the Wives within the home and by the Aunts in other areas of society. Which features of this women's culture would appeal to feminists? Which features would horrify feminists?

Pornography is another word that is difficult to define. Some definitions state that pornography is any media or behaviour that is degrading to women. Atwood demonstrates that treating women as reproductive objects is degrading. In this respect *The Handmaid's Tale* has been criticised by some as pornographic. In the 1980s some feminist organisations were aligning themselves with anti-pornography Christian fundamentalists, although the two groups had very different ideas about abortion and women's rights. Atwood explores the complexities of this trend for women through the creation of Gilead. Ultimately all women lose more than they gain. *The Handmaid's Tale* was first published in 1985. Which feminist and anti-feminist issues are still of concern today?

Social, historical context

Social, historical and cultural context

This novel is a seminal text in Atwood's canon of work because of the social, historical and cultural strains intertwined to produce the Republic of Gilead. In many ways the futuristic society presented is a hark back to societal conditions throughout history. The twentieth century has been an anomaly is terms of individual rights and freedoms: prior to the twentieth century, the majority of the population could not read; in law women were treated as men's property. For centuries the Church controlled the state. Procreation was crucial to survival because of the high infant mortality rate and lower life expectancy. Society had stricter agreed moral values, and there was more obvious racism. Freedom and equality are products of the twentieth century. Gilead is therefore a futuristic society deeply rooted in the past. As Offred says, 'It's only the more recent history that offends them'. Ironically it was through the church, not the state, in the nineteenth century that many people were taught to read in order to read the Bible.

Some aspects of the social, historical and cultural context have been covered separately, such as feminism. Another aspect of the historical context of the novel is the founding of the United States. Followers of the Puritan religion who sailed on the Mayflower established the first successful settlement in America. Puritans had strict moral discipline and religious values. The founding Pilgrim Fathers originally left England to practise their non–conformist religion free of persecution and to be free of what they saw as lax religious values at the time. They regarded luxury, pleasure and social indulgence as sinful. The Puritans originally used the birthing stool used during Janine's delivery.

Puritanism is the historical religious influence in Gilead, and the rise of fundamentalism is a contemporary religious influence in the United States. Fundamentalists promote traditional family values, and are abhorrently anti-abortionist and anti-homosexual. Some fundamentalists have formed para-military militias. The rise of the political right in America is reflected in the capitalist spirit of the Commanders.

The novel is also set against the context of slavery in the United States. Being a Handmaid or a Martha is a form of slavery. The Handmaids' patronymics define them as property of the Commanders. Like the slaves, they are separated from their own birth families, and escaped Handmaids are severely physically punished. The cultural issue of racism is evident in the relocation of the sons of Ham, and the declining Caucasian birth rate.

The effects of late twentieth-century environmental issues, such as toxic poisoning and the depletion of marine life for commercial purposes, play a part in the creation of Gilead. Environmentally hazardous areas, the Colonies, are the punitive destination for older women, barren Handmaids and homosexuals.

Narrative technique

Narrative style, structure and technique

A level students find that the narrative style, structure and technique of *The Handmaid's Tale* pose the greatest difficulties in studying the novel. In terms of style, Atwood draws from a mosaic of narrative genres. There are elements of fictive autobiography, dystopian science fiction and romance.

The narrative structure proves initially unwieldy because fragments of three stories are being told at once. The opening sections supply details of life at the Red Centre and the daily domestic routine of a Handmaid. Much of the situation described is confusing and unfamiliar to us, thus initially giving us the impression that the story is set far in the future. As we read through the novel, the setting becomes increasingly familiar, thereby shifting our perception of the time period the story is set in to closer to the present. The reason for the complex structure is that Offred's story has been fragmented and pieced together by Professor Pieixoto.

The story of the third placement begins with the mundane details of Offred's life and surroundings. Look at how much attention is given to the description of her room in Chapter 2. Due to her lack of freedom, her life is monotonous and uneventful. Her imagination, however, is still free, so she creates a secret life of sensory perceptions and memories to survive the boredom. To prisoners the change of light throughout the day, or a visit from an insect can arouse wonder and intrigue.

Professor Pieixoto is frustrated by Offred's account because it includes few facts about the war. This is partly because she does not have access to this information. More importantly, Offred offers an alternative perception of the regime. She tells the story of the oppressed and powerless, which would disagree greatly with any official versions of life during the period of the Gileadean Republic. Whose firsthand accounts of events throughout history remain untold?

Offred's narrative structure is well balanced. Atwood subtly prepares us for most events throughout the novel. Reread the introductions of Serena Joy, Chapter 3, Nick, Chapter 4, and Ofglen, Chapter 4. Which details resurface later in the story?

Atwood uses flashbacks. Which sections are particularly reliant on flashbacks, and why? The narrative also switches effortlessly, and at times without warning, between the present, recent past and distant past. Often the present narrative is informed by the past. 'My red shoes are off, my legs tucked up underneath me on the chair, surrounded by a buttress of red skirt, ... as at a campfire, of earlier and more picnic days.' Offred is like the palimpsest, a parchment that is scraped clean in order to be reused, but with traces of the former text visible underneath. 'Traces' of her original identity and beliefs exist underneath her Handmaid guise. Find other examples of the past transcending the present narrative.

Offred's story is a dialogue with the audience. She is a self-conscious narrator who is aware of the limitations of narrating reality and the human need for telling stories. She involves the audience in her dialogue by direct address, anticipating our response and justifying some of her actions to us. Professor Pieixoto continues her dialogue when he asks for questions.

The Historical Notes are written in a completely different narrative style. Pieixoto addresses a live audience.

The tone of his narrative is academic, prosaic and objective. His entire narrative is a reconstruction of Offred's story from an empowered male perspective. His emphasis on fact and authority silences Offred's voice.

In her narrative Offred relates the stories of many women: her mother, Moira, Serena Joy and to a lesser extent, Janine. Compare the stories of female characters to the stories of male characters. We learn much more about the women because Offred's tapes give a voice to a group of people that had no voice. Whose story is Professor Pieixoto concerned with? Apart from Ofglen, we do not know how any of the characters' stories finished, only that they would have all been dead by the time of the Twelfth Symposium. Each of these characters' stories bears relevance to contemporary society so, to a certain extent, their stories are not finished.

Language

Language

The language is at once accessible and inaccessible. The vocabulary, syntax and semantics are modern and familiar, making the language seem deceptively easy. Atwood's many allusions to literary and cultural sources, however, demand a high degree of cultural literacy. Many of the literary allusions occur in Aunt Lydia's teachings, where she outrageously distorts the original text. References are made to the Bible, mythology, Karl Marx, Sigmund Freud, René Descartes, Charles Darwin, Napoleon, Shakespeare, Milton, Chaucer and fairy-tales. There are contemporary cultural references to anthropology, environmental issues, feminism, films, Islamic traditions, religious fundamentalism, sociology, and technology. Historical references are made to slavery, painting, sculpture, American Puritanism and Nazism. There are musical references to hymns, folk songs, Beethoven, Elvis Presley, Mantovani and popular music of the 1980s. In the Scrabble game, Offred uses many biological words. Atwood invents many neologisms, the meaning of which we must guess at, such as Econowives, Prayvaganzas, Salvagings, and Particicution.

Offred enjoys word play and often contemplates the multiple meanings of words and phrases. A variety of speech patterns are used. Compare and contrast the speech of the following characters: Offred, the Commander, Moira, Offred's mother, Rita, Cora, the television broadcaster and Professor Pieixoto. Compare Offred's spoken language as a Handmaid to the language of her memories.

The significance of language in shaping experience is also a theme in the novel. The official patriarchal language of the Republic stands in direct contrast to Offred's private feminine language of love, emotion, flowers, colour and the body.

Imagery and motifs

Imagery and motifs

The motifs of flowers, doubles, eyes, missing persons and ghosts run throughout the novel.

Flowers are represented in a painting in Offred's bedroom. The flowers in Serena Joy's garden represent Offred. The garden is important to Serena Joy and Offred. Like Offred herself, the flowers are subversive and a reproach to the Commander's Wife in their ability to be fruitful.

Offred leads a double life: one physical and linear; one in memory and sensation which is fluid and non-linear. Offred has two identities: one as a Handmaid; one as a wife, mother, daughter, friend and career woman. Offred has two names: her Gileadean patronymic; and her birth name, which she never shares with us. Offred knows that she and Ofglen look like doubles as they shop. Many characters have counterparts: Nick and Luke; Moira and Ofglen; Offred and the previous Offred. Offred's position as the Commander's mistress parallels her position as 'the other woman' before Luke's divorce.

The Eyes of the Lord are the secret police in Gilead. Other than when she is in her room, Offred knows that she is being watched. She also comments on several characters' eyes. The hole in her ceiling where the chandelier was now looks like an eye.

Offred's narrative is full of missing persons and ghosts. Some are found (Moira and her daughter) and some remain missing (Luke and her mother). Her predecessor haunts Offred, and Offred is a ghost to her daughter. Others, such as Nick, the Commander and Ofglen are missing a pre-Gileadean existence. Offred herself becomes a missing person.

There is much Victorian imagery. The Commander lives in a Victorian house. In many ways Gilead is a neo-Victorian society. Offred also uses much bodily imagery, especially as an alternative and interior landscape. There are also many references to the moon. In Roman mythology Diana was the goddess of chastity and the moon. Why is this symbolism relevant to Offred?

Examiner's tips

Examination

Coursework

These icons are used throughout the **Text commentary** to highlight key points in the text, provide advice on avoiding common errors and offer useful hints on thoroughly preparing yourself for coursework and examination essays on this novel.

Although the tips are specified as being relevant to *either* a coursework essay *or* an examination essay, many of them are applicable to both.

■ Text commentary

The epigraphs

An epigraph is a quotation at the beginning of a work of literature. An epigraph usually directs the reader towards some of the themes of the writing. *The Handmaid's Tale* is prefaced by three quotations, each presenting an idea explored in the novel.

The first quotation is taken from Genesis, 30:1–3. It is the biblical authority from which the Republic of Gilead borrowed the idea of using Handmaids to bear children for barren wives. The phrase 'Give me children, or else I die.' is repeated twice in the course of the novel. Whereas Rachel made the original command as a threat to Jacob, for Offred it serves as a threatening axiom. Gilead decrees that Handmaids who fail to conceive after three attempts will be sent to the Colonies to clean up toxic waste. The life expectancy of colonials is only a few years due to the fatal health hazards posed.

The second quotation comes from Jonathan Swift's satirical piece *A Modest Proposal*. This pamphlet, published in 1729, is one of the best examples of satire in the English language. Swift outrageously proposes that starvation in Ireland can be remedied by rearing Irish infants as livestock to be eaten. This epigraph suggests that the story can be approached as a satirical response to political issues of the late twentieth century.

The third quotation is a Sufi proverb about survival. One must do whatever it takes to survive. Can you think of any alternative interpretations?

Part I Night

Chapter 1

Details of the sleeping accommodation at the Red Centre are introduced.

'We slept in what had once been the gymnasium.'

Narrative technique

Do not be alarmed if you are confused after reading this introductory chapter. Atwood deliberately manipulates the sense of time in this novel, and many ideas of time are presented here. The story opens in the recent past and recalls a more distant past. How far in the future is the story set? A sense of rapidly changing times is communicated through changing female fashions. In the distant past, the narrator 'yearned for the future'. How does Atwood create the impression that the narrator now yearns for the past?

The narrative is also confusing because the narrator is unnamed. Which details gradually identify the narrator as female? The narrator is deliberately ambiguous about details of her present situation. What we are not told is as important as what we are told, for instance in what situations are large buildings such as gymnasiums converted into makeshift accommodation for large numbers of people? What might this suggest about the situation presented?

It is ironic that what used to be a gymnasium in the past, a place of activity,

---

Coursework

The opening chapter of any novel is extremely important because it sets the scene and tone, introduces some of the main characters, starts the action, introduces a central conflict and introduces some of the main themes. When answering questions about the opening scene, be specific about the purposes achieved in this chapter.

A popular essay question on *The Handmaid's Tale* focuses on the complex structure of the novel. Pay particular attention to the titles of each part, and the arrangement of parts entitled Night. Why is this first part called Night?

See Question 1, page 62.

Imagery and motifs

is now used as a dormitory, a place of inactivity. The references to games, dances, sex and high emotion in the past are contrasted by the regimented life that exists now. What details suggest order and force? Keep track of the distinction between imagery associated with the past and the imagery associated with the present in this chapter. The society, although not named until Chapter 5, is The Republic of Gilead. The gymnasium the narrator speaks of is part of the Rachel and Leah Re-education Centre, named in Chapter 17. The narrator and her peers nickname it 'The Red Centre' because the colour red marks their function in society in the form of their uniforms, and they are prepared at the centre for their new role in society. (For ease of reference in this Guide the centre will be referred to as the Red Centre.) This brief introduction to the Red Centre prepares us for the ideology and structure of Gileadean society.

Dystopian literature

Details such as army cots and blankets, armed guards, and 'Aunts' patrolling with electric cattle prods create a sinister atmosphere. Although we do not know the name or location of this future society, the tone and imagery identify that this is a dystopian society based on force and brutality. A power hierarchy is evident: the guards are a special group within 'the Angels', and they have power over the Aunts; the Aunts have power over the narrator and her equals. Men and women are segregated and human interaction is forbidden. The Angels, although more powerful than the narrator's group, must not look during the women's walk around the grounds of the complex.

The seeds of resistance, however, are also introduced. The narrator and her equals have found alternative ways of communicating. They even think about ways of bargaining with the Angels.

'Aunt Sara and Aunt Elizabeth patrolled; they had electric cattle prods slung on thongs from their leather belts.'

Atwood's novels are rich in word play. This is especially obvious in her ironic

Language

choice of names for the various roles in this futuristic society: the armed guards are called 'Angels'; the endearing term 'Aunt' refers to women who keep order with electric cattle prods.

There are many examples of Atwood's precise choice of words. 'Electric cattle prods' are instruments of control that were used by American police during the civil rights demonstrations of the 1960s. The women are not at the centre by choice and may try to riot or rebel. This association also suggests that the Aunts treat the other women like cattle. What other activities are associated with cattle?

Examination

Coursework

Examination and coursework essays frequently focus on the significance of imagery. Pay attention to other examples of cattle imagery.

Part II Shopping

Chapter 2

The narrator describes the house and the routines where she presently resides.

The narrative structure of this novel is complex. The narrator tells us three

Narrative technique

stories at once. The tale opens with a fragment of the story of her 're-education' at the Red Centre following the creation of the Republic of Gilead. Part II thrusts us into present time where the narrator is in her current position as a Handmaid at the Commander's house. Interwoven into these two narratives is the story of what the narrator refers to as 'the time before'. Pay particular attention to the shifts in verb tense between, and within, chapters.

Much of the opening chapters of the novel is concerned with sensory observations. The narrator shares her interior monologue of initial observations with the reader because communication with others in the house is discouraged. The tone is casual and detached.

'Thinking can hurt your chances, and I intend to last.'

Offred

Although the narrator remains unnamed, she confides to us that she intends to survive her present imprisonment. The narrator's Handmaid name is revealed as Offred in Chapter 24. (For ease of reference she will be referred to in this Guide by her Handmaid's name.) As she describes the house she now lives in, her sense of isolation under this new regime is more intense than it was at the Centre. The bedroom has minimal furniture. There are no methods of escape from her room – even through suicide. She is lonely and longs to gossip with Rita and Cora. The collective defiance of the previous chapter is no longer available to her, so she will have to fight for her survival alone. The only instrument of resistance available to her is her memory. Her memories of her past are crucial to her retaining her former identity.

'Waste not want not. I am not being wasted. Why do I want?'

Language

Offred contemplates the power of words through their multiple associations. What used to be a game that she played with her husband Luke, is now an important means of Offred's self-preservation against the dogma of society. The theme of the power of language figures prominently. Offred's memories of 'the time before' are littered with images of freedom. Language, too, was used much more freely then. Pay close attention to the subtle differences in the language Offred uses in her memories, when thinking about her present situation and in conversation with others. Find other examples of word play.

Atwood draws upon a rich diversity of language in her novels. Keep track of the varieties of language presented throughout the novel. Rita and Cora's speech is characteristic of small town America. It tells us a great deal about their age and education. An absence of language is also apparent in the use of pictorial shopping tokens instead of a shopping list.

Imagery and motifs

The power hierarchy of society identifies the various groups only by their clothing. Clothing defines a person's function in society. Function rather than individuality is valued. In this chapter we are introduced to more groups within the society: Commanders, Commander's Wives and Marthas. Women who do not serve a purpose are 'Unwomen' and are banished from the society to the undesirable 'Colonies'. The conversation between Rita and Cora suggests that the narrator's function is connected with reproduction. Which details suggest this?

Details of the style and colour of clothing are significant and contradictory. The narrator's dress is similar to that of a nun, only in red, a colour associated with prostitution. Offred sums this up as 'A Sister, dipped in blood'. What other ideas are associated with this image? How is Offred's association with nuns further reinforced? Like a nun, a Handmaid has to give up her identity and family.

Gilead is a fundamentalist Christian society. The first indication that this is a religious society is the reference to a nunnery. The second indication is the association of the name Martha. Martha was a woman who served Jesus through housework. See Luke 10:38–42.

Although it has yet to be formally identified, the setting for this society is on the north-eastern coast of America. These states were originally British colonies. Explain the irony of undesirables now being banished from this area to 'the Colonies'.

Chapter 3

Offred's introduction and flashback to meeting the Commander's Wife.

Offred takes us through her daily routine, moving from inside the

Commander's house to the garden. She is sensitive to the beauty, sensuality and vitality of the flowers. This is a recurring motif throughout the novel. The garden is, however, 'the domain of the Commander's Wife'. The irony of the barren Wife tending to her fruitful garden as a surrogate child,

Imagery and motifs

'something for them to order and maintain and care for', is not lost on Offred. The flowers represent femininity. Offred identifies her former self with the flowers, particularly the tulips which 'are red, a darker crimson towards the stem, as if they had been cut and are beginning to heal there.'

'I am a reproach to her; and a necessity.'

Some of the pieces of the narrative puzzle are beginning to fall to into place.

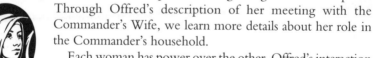

Through Offred's description of her meeting with the Commander's Wife, we learn more details about her role in the Commander's household.

Each woman has power over the other. Offred's interaction is characterised by the behaviour and language of an inferior.

Offred

Serena Joy, however, is unnerved by Offred's presence. Offred has no power of authority in this society, but she still has the inner power of her former identity. Her defiance is demonstrated in her precise observation and unsympathetic description of the older woman's appearance. Serena Joy's appearance is characteristic of women who appeared on evangelical American television programmes in the 1970s and 1980s. What does this suggest about Serena Joy's religious convictions during 'the time before'?

Gilead is a patriarchal society. Women within the society, regardless of status, hold little power. It is interesting to note that the Commander's Wife

Women and feminism

is introduced before the Commander. This story, however, is told from the perspective of a woman. We have been introduced to most of the alternatives for women in Gilead: Wives, Aunts, Handmaids, Marthas and Unwomen. What does this tell us about how women are valued? Why might the Commander's Wife be more important in Offred's life than the Commander?

Chapter 4

Offred continues on her daily trip to the shops accompanied by another Handmaid.

Language

The names of the cars, Whirlwind, Chariot and Behemoth are all taken from the Bible. Further biblical allusions are evident in Aunt Lydia's teaching and the conversation between the two Handmaids.

The reasons behind the formation of Gilead are gradually revealed. Gilead is fighting a religious war. The details of the barrier and Offred's mistrust of others suggest Gilead was created as the result of a military coup. Two of the Gileadean rituals introduced in this chapter are plays on words. 'Prayvaganzas' is a play on 'prayer' and 'extravaganza'. This suggests prayer meetings as a form of lavish entertainment. 'Salvagings' is an ironic play on the words 'savaging' and 'salvation'. A Salvaging must be a form of public execution that is justified by the state as a form of salvation for the good of the Republic. What do the names of these rituals suggest about the religious activities in Gilead?

Offred

Sexual behaviour is taboo in Gilead. Offred's description of the Commander's Guardian Nick, however, is sexually charged. Like Offred, Nick appears to be subtly rebellious in the face of the restrictions imposed on him, but it is too soon for her to tell whether he is like-minded or a member of the informant group 'The Eyes'.

'I enjoy the power; power of a dog bone, passive but there.'

Offred is aware of women's former sexual power over men and swings her hips defiantly. This concluding paragraph can be read in two ways: Offred could be condemning the unnatural restrictions placed on men in Gilead; equally she could be condemning the men's view of women as sex objects in 'the time before'. How does Offred implicitly reveal that she is a Handmaid?

Examination

Candidates have to be able to demonstrate that they understand multiple meanings. Note alternative interpretations of language and events throughout the novel.

Chapter 5

Offred and Ofglen visit the shops in the heart of Gilead.

'There are no lawyers any more, and the university is closed.'

A lack of justice and a lack of education are popular mechanisms for control in dystopias.

Women and feminism

At the heart of Gileadean society is the responsibility to protect women. Compare the lack of 'freedom from' in the time before to the apparent 'freedom from' sexual crimes in Gilead. In effect women have freedom from choices, which is not a freedom at all.

Coursework

Many alternative models of women are presented in this novel. Offred longs to see her friend Moira. Moira will emerge as an important alternative model of women in the time before, just as Ofglen provides an alternative model of a Handmaid. What alternative models of women do a) Ofwarren and b) the Japanese women provide? Keep track of the various models of women presented. See Question 2, page 63.

Language

There are many biblical allusions in the names of places in Gilead. Gilead, itself, is a biblical reference to the mountain in Genesis where the patriarch Jacob flees with his family. Read the story of Jacob; then read Hosea 6:8. Why is the name Gilead appropriate?

The names of the shops also come from the Bible. There are many references to 'all flesh'. In the book of Isaiah the term refers to all of humanity. Isaiah 40:6 says 'All flesh is grass, and all the goodliness thereof is as the flower of the field'. This same idea is repeated in Peter 1:24, 'For all flesh is as grass, and all the glory of man as the flower of grass. The grass withereth, and the flower thereof falleth away.' Relate these references to Gileadean ideology.

Explain Atwood's word play in the statement, 'Habits are hard to break'.

Chapter 6

The Handmaids observe the victims of a Men's Salvaging on The Wall.

'Inside it you can see paintings, of women in long sombre dresses, their hair covered by white caps, and of upright men, darkly clothed and unsmiling.'

This is a reference to the Pilgrim Fathers who came over to America in the Mayflower. America was colonised by members of Christian sects fleeing from persecution. Puritans wore black, were teetotal, believed in hard work and rejected entertainment such as the theatre and dancing.

'It's only the more recent history that offends them.'

There have been many references to the Victorians: another patriarchal society that 'protected' women. Why does this society find contemporary history from the 1960s onwards offensive? What values shifted at this time?

Social, historical context

Atwood draws on many historical, societal and cultural traditions in this novel. The witch hunts of Old Salem are recalled in the description of the witch hunts taking place through the medical profession in Gilead. The rule of 'evidence from a single woman is no longer admissible' comes from Islam. Identify links between Gileadean and strict Islamic society.

Part III Night

Chapter 7

Lying in bed at night, Offred steps out of the present into her memories of Moira, her mother and her daughter.

Women and feminism

As she is not allowed to write, Offred's resistance is through her thoughts. How does her distinction between 'lie' and 'lay' reinforce her will to survive? Explain Offred's play on words in 'Date Rape'.

Offred's mother was involved with the American feminist movement of the late 1960s and early 1970s. What were the women protesting against at this book burning?

Narrative technique

The structure of Offred's family's escape from Gilead is of great significance. It begins with the immediate after effects of Offred's capture. Think of the narrative structure as a camera lens zoomed in on an image and gradually widening out to let more detail in.

Notice the shifts in this chapter from the present to the past, and back to the present. When do these shifts occur in the narrative?

Explain the narrative significance of Offred's comments on storytelling at the end of the chapter: 'I would like to believe this is a story I'm telling.'

Coursework

Make notes about Offred's comments on the storytelling process. Consider why she needs to tell her story and how stories shape our experiences. See Question 1, page 62.

Part IV Waiting Room

Chapter 8

The next day, Offred receives a signal from Ofglen.

Offred

The narrative offers two hints in this chapter that Offred's life might become more interesting. Firstly Ofglen uses the password of the Mayday resistance movement: 'It's a beautiful May day.' How does this shed new light on how Ofglen has been presented so far? Secondly, the Commander tries to see Offred's face. Why is this significant?

'This is a treacherous smell, and I know I must shut it out.'

The smell of baking bread is treachery because it is a direct link to the time before, as are the blue and white striped dishtowels that Rita wipes her hands on. When Offred starts to think, 'things haven't changed that much', she has to catch herself because she knows that these are meaningless details, and she is seeing them out of context.

At the end of the chapter she refers to the bedroom as 'my room'. Luckily she notices her mistake.

'The tulips along the border are redder than ever, opening, no longer winecups but chalices; thrusting themselves up, to what end?'

Imagery and motifs

The tulips seem to symbolise Offred. Where else in this chapter is the tulip motif apparent? There are many domestic images, such as those mentioned above, in this chapter. How are these images contrasted against the daily suffering and oppression experienced in Gilead?

Women and feminism

One of the ideas that Atwood is examining in this novel is the extremes of both the women's movement and the anti-women's movement. Serena Joy, although a career woman, was against the women's movement. Offred observes the irony of Serena Joy's loss of independent status and frustration at staying at home, which was exactly the ideal she used to preach: 'How frustrated she must be, now that she's been taken at her word.' Atwood's point is that women must be careful of losing their choices, whatever their cause.

Chapter 9

Offred claims her room as her own space. She recalls her initial examination of the room and the message she uncovered from a previous Handmaid.

Offred

The previous chapter closes with Offred correcting her lapse of thinking of the bedroom as her room. She begins this chapter by claiming the room as her private space: 'My room, then.' She also introduces one of the many references to a waiting room in Part IV. In what sense is her bedroom a waiting room?

'Old love; there's no other kind of love in this room now.'

The exciting memory of her clandestine rendezvous with Luke in a hotel room is in stark contrast to her functional experience of sex during the Ceremony. Old love is the expression of love through sexual intercourse. This kind of love no longer exists in Gilead. How is it subtly hinted that Offred's predecessor committed suicide?

'*Nolite te bastardes carborundorum.*'

This is a pseudo-Latin expression made up by schoolboys, meaning 'Don't let the bastards get you down.' The Commander translates its meaning for Offred in Chapter 29. Offred's discovery of the message left for her from her predecessor becomes central to her personal resistance movement. She feels a spiritual connection to her predecessor and she feels solidarity between herself, the former Offred and Moira.

Chapter 10

Still in her room, Offred reminisces about her college days.

Women and feminism

Being an Aunt is another role that women can take in Gileadean society. What impression have you formed of Aunt Lydia so far? What kind of women are Aunts?

Offred and Serena Joy each sometimes think about songs from the time before. Contrast the songs Offred sings with Serena Joy's recordings.

What point do you think Atwood is trying to make in juxtaposing Moira's idea for an 'underwhore party' beside Offred's memories of reports of sexual assaults against women in the time before?

Chapter 11

Offred recounts her previous day's visit to the doctor.

'*Give me children, or else I die.*'

Narrative technique

Read this passage taken from Genesis 30:1 to learn more about the biblical basis for the Handmaids. In this section Offred is waiting for the 'Ceremony', where she will have intercourse with the Commander. She is unsettled by the choice of salvation the doctor offers her. She knows that she has less than two years to become pregnant, or else she will be declared an Unwoman and sent to the Colonies. How is tension built up in this chapter?

Why is this chapter placed here? How does it add to the sense of waiting that Atwood is creating in this section? How does the narrative in this chapter reinforce Offred's function as 'vessel for procreation'?

Although the narrative is told from the first person point of view, Offred can see herself from the point of view of others. Which details in this chapter are described from the doctor's perspective? Keep track of descriptions of Offred from other people's perspectives. See Question 1, page 62.

Coursework

Chapter 12

Offred has her bath in preparation for the Ceremony.

Offred contemplates both her present and past identities. In her present identity she is a prisoner of her body. What details reinforce this? Her body is being cleaned and purified before the Ceremony. During the bath she disassociates her body from her mind, and thinks about her daughter. When describing bathing her baby daughter, a time of mother and child bonding, her language is emotive and tactile, 'I put my face against the soft hair at the back of her neck and breathe her in…'. Her present bath is merely functional, as reinforced in the sterile imagery, 'totally clean, germless, without bacteria, like the surface of the moon.'

'What I must present is a made thing, not something born.'

Offred's narrative has been building up to the Ceremony, which will take place that night. She imagines the anticipation is equally tense for the Wife. Her closing statement refers to a feminist writer who argues that woman is made rather than born. A Handmaid is not inherently valuable to society. They are made valuable by conceiving. With this in mind, find an alternative meaning for her comment, 'I compose myself'.

■ Self-test questions Chapters 1–12

Who? What? Why? When? Where? How?

1 Why does Offred refuse to refer to the bedroom she sleeps in as 'my room' in Chapter 2?
2 Who lives in the Colonies?
3 How long has Offred been at the Commander's house?
4 What are 'Econowives'?

5 Where do Offred and Ofglen go every day on their way home from the shops?
6 What is Gender Treachery?
7 How long does a Handmaid posting last?
8 What choice does the doctor offer Offred?
9 How long has it been since Offred has seen her daughter?
10 Why do Handmaids have a tattoo on their ankles?

Prove it
Provide textual evidence for the following statements.
1 Offred is sexually attracted to Nick.
2 This is not Offred's first posting as a Handmaid.
3 The traditional fields of law, education, medicine and science are not valued in Gilead.
4 Offred refuses to believe that Luke is dead.
5 Moira and Offred were at the Red Centre together.
6 Many Handmaids have committed suicide.
7 Offred worries that her generation's sexual irresponsibility contributed to the loss of sexual freedom in Gilead.
8 There were signs that women needed to be protected before the creation of the Republic of Gilead.
9 Offred feels frustrated.
10 Moira is unconventional.

What is the significance?
Identify the speaker, the context of the passage and its significance.
1 'As far as I'm concerned, this is like a business transaction.'
2 'A return to traditional values.'
3 'Gilead is within you.'
4 'It has taken so little time to change our minds, about things like this.'
5 'The difference between *lie* and *lay*.'
6 'She could get one of those over her head, he'd say.'
7 'How frustrated she must be, now that she's been taken at her word.'
8 'I thought it was an isolated incident, at the time.'
9 'I compose myself.'
10 'Blessed are the meek. She didn't go on to say anything about inheriting the earth.'

Part V Nap

Chapter 13

Offred has a nap before the Ceremony. Moving from consciousness to unconsciousness, her thoughts oscillate between the present, the Red Centre and the past.

Offred's new perception of nineteenth-century 'erotic' paintings, that 'They were paintings about boredom', demonstrates how intangible cultural reference points are. Cultural products are analysed and valued according to the ideology of the culture engaged in the analysis. This episode anticipates the academic analysis of Offred's narrative in the Historical Notes.

'*Her* fault, *her* fault, *her* fault, we chant in unison.'

Social, historical context

In the 1980s, some criminological theories hypothesised that victims were as much to blame for the crimes against them as the criminals. This branch of criminal psychology was often cited in cases of sexual assault against women. It was believed that women provoked men into committing sexual crimes against them by wearing provocative clothing or inviting men back to their homes for coffee. In the legal proceedings, the women were often put on trial to prove their innocence, rather than the sexual offender.

Imagery and motifs

Due to her physical restrictions, Offred's body has become her new frontier to explore from the inside. She describes the sensations inside her body with the geographical terminology of dangerous terrain and unpredictable climate: swamp, fenland, treacherous ground. Her body is treacherous, as it wholly determines her future. She likens her reproductive system to a universe, with her vagina at its centre. Her menstrual cycle has become a lunar orbit. Why is this imagery fitting?

Determine the meaning of her dream about Luke by analysing the imagery. Offred's dream about her failed escape from Gilead with her daughter is the worst because they were so close to freedom. The idea of failed escape is introduced in this chapter through Moira's introduction to the Red Centre.

Part VI Household

Chapter 14

The household gathers for the preliminary prayers.

Social, historical context

Offred first remarks on the Commander's wealth and then describes the paintings of Pilgrim Mothers as an affected touch to suggest pious ancestry. The Pilgrims were prosperous and came to see poverty as a sign of God's disfavour. The Protestant work ethic gave rise to capitalism. How does the order of Offred's impressions reveal her view of Puritanism?

'Resettlement of the Children of Ham is continuing on schedule'

Dystopian literature

Ham is a black man from the Book of Genesis. Not only is Gilead a racist society, it also practices religious intolerance. An utopian society is characterised by equality. How many forms of inequality exist in Gilead? Gilead is a modern society in reverse in that it is recreating the religious intolerance that the original Puritans came to America to escape.

'it's the Montreal satellite station, being blocked.'

Dystopian societies block out external information. Notice how the news reports only near victories for Gilead. Dystopian societies rely on propaganda to control society. The news reports, although undemocratic, give us a clearer picture of the size and location of Gilead through mention of the borders being defended. Re-read this section while looking at a map of the United States to get a better idea of Gilead's territory.

Narrative technique

We learn in this chapter that Offred is not the narrator's real name. In fact we never learn either her or her daughter's names. The reason for withholding this information will not become clear until the Historical Notes. Why might she be reluctant to tell us her real name?

The story of Offred's failed escape and capture is narrated in reverse. What is the effect of telling the story from the consequences to the beginning, instead of vice versa? Re-read Chapters 7 and 13. Why is the narrative style becoming less intense? What do you expect to learn next about the failed escape?

Examination

This section is entitled Household. Explore the multiple meanings of this word contemplated by Offred in this chapter. Look for connotations of this word throughout this section, and think of other associations with the words house and hold.

Chapter 15

The prayers before the Ceremony.

We are unable to form a clear picture of the Commander. His changing appearance reinforces Offred's ambivalent feelings towards him.

Narrative technique

Again the narrative weaves seamlessly between the immediate present and the recent past at the Red Centre. Offred thinks of Moira and her predecessor in the house when she needs the spirit of resistance. In fact, she envisions her predecessor to be Moira. What does Moira mean to Offred? How is the atmosphere made more intense?

Notice how subtly Atwood structures Offred's narrative. During the silent prayer Offred thinks of her predecessor's message because she cannot pray. Then she recalls the consequences of Moira's unsuccessful attempted escape. We find out that Moira was punished by electrocution to her feet. The feet were chosen because they bear no importance on her function as a Handmaid. Offred cannot pray to a God that allows her fellow man to use torture, and devalue women as second class citizens.

'I've got my eye on you.'

Offred cleverly plays with perspective and power. During the prayers she has become the Eyes watching the Commander. This is part of Offred's silent rebellion during the prayers. Link

Coursework this alternative perspective with Offred's alternative internal frontier presented in Chapter 13. These are both good examples of feminist writing where an alternative female code is created in contrast to the traditional code of binary oppositions. See Question 2, page 63.

Chapter 16

The Ceremony.

'Kissing is forbidden between us. This makes it bearable.'

There are no flashbacks in this chapter. It is a short chapter to emphasise the

Women and feminism

brevity and functional nature of the relationship between the Commander, his Wife and Offred. Offred explains cogently that this act is not love, copulation or rape. How does she highlight that this act is being done to her rather than with her? Even in the one form of sexual relationship that is permitted, Handmaids have no power. Does Serena Joy contribute to the violation against Offred, or is she equally violated?

Chapter 17

Offred puts her rebellion into action. She steals a daffodil from the living-room and has a long embrace with Nick.

'I want to steal something.'

This statement sums up her thirst for rebellion in this chapter. Firstly, her act

Offred

of 'stealing' the butter for her face is more than a mere act of vanity: the Wives forbid moisturiser, so 'buttering' her face is an act of rebellion against the Wives. She also imagines herself in collusion with Moira and her predecessor, 'My predecessor in this room, my friend with the freckles and the good laugh, must have done this too, this buttering.' As we have seen

before, these Handmaids' acts of rebellion have become a talisman for Offred. She breaks the rules of the house by going into the living-room. She steals the daffodil in order to leave it as a message for her replacement. Again, communication between Handmaids is not allowed, so that her reason for stealing the daffodil is an even greater act of defiance than the physical acquisition. Most significantly she 'steals' an embrace with Nick, which is completely forbidden. She is even tempted to have sex with him right there in the sitting-room. Not only does she break Gileadean law by physical contact with Nick; she is also betraying Luke. How does she think Luke would feel about her 'relationship' with Nick?

This chapter is sexually charged. Atwood prepares us for the exciting

Narrative technique

climax of the kiss through the narrative. Offred is restless when she returns to her room. It is night-time. She looks at the moon and is overcome by her desire for Luke. She takes a risk and goes downstairs to commit a forbidden act. Tension is created as we anticipate her discovery. Our fears are heightened when, in the dark, she knocks something. She is discovered, but her discovery turns into an even greater punishable offence. The embrace with Nick relieves her sexual frustration, and at the same time leaves her hungry for more. At the end of the chapter she is drunk with desire for Nick, 'I find the door, turn the knob, fingers on cool porcelain, open. It's all I can do.' Our curiosity is also aroused by the message from the Commander.

Atwood infuses the scene in the parlour with sexual tension through the use of the present tense, short sentences and Offred's interior monologue contrasted by the brief verbal exchanges between her and Nick. Look carefully at the imagery used in this scene. In how many ways are Offred and Nick both mirrors and magnets?

Part VII Night

Chapter 18

In bed, Offred considers in turn the possibilities that Luke is dead, that Luke is a prisoner and that Luke made it safely to Canada and, as part of the resistance movement, will rescue her.

'In hope.'

Offred's intimacy with Nick sparks off thoughts about Luke. Offred has

Offred

imagined three versions of Luke's fate so that she is prepared for the truth if and when she learns it. Most importantly she retains her hope. Her hope that one day she will be loved again by Luke is vital to her survival. She even has hopes for him in the worst of scenarios. If he is dead, she hopes that he died quickly and with minimal pain. If he is in prison, she hopes that they can communicate by thought transference. What details from the television news are evident in her version of Luke's successful escape? Through Offred's three versions we also discover more details about Luke's appearance and the family's failed escape.

Part VIII Birth Day

Chapter 19

The birth mobile takes Offred to the birth of Ofwarren's baby.

'HOPE and CHARITY, where have they been stowed?'

Dystopian literature

The words on the set of cushions refers to I Corinthians 13:13. It is possible that Rita and Cora have the other cushions. It is also possible that only the Faith cushion remains, because the other two virtues are not valued in Gilead. Where did Offred mention that hope existed in Gilead in the last chapter? Charity is the greatest of these virtues, but like so many other ideas, it is not practised in Gilead.

Not only is Gilead flawed morally, it suffers from terrible ecological problems. We learn in this chapter some more reasons for the formation of the Republic, and an explanation of why Handmaids are necessary – the environment became toxic from pollution. Clearly the chemical excess of the late twentieth century have taken their toll, especially on the birth rate of healthy babies. We now understand better the doctor's comment in Chapter 11 that most of the Commanders are sterile. A dystopian society is one that does not satisfy the needs of its members. Given that the birth rate is below the line of replacement, the Republic is inherently flawed in that it could die out. There is another point to consider: to what extent was 'the time before' a dystopia? Agent Orange was a chemical used by the Americans in Vietnam. It was blamed for later human biological problems.

'*I will greatly multiply thy sorrow and thy conception; in sorrow thou shalt bring forth children.*'

Women and feminism

This chapter presents the argument between hospital birth and natural childbirth. The biblical quote is from Genesis 3:16. In this passage Eve is given pain in childbirth as her punishment for eating the forbidden fruit. Natural childbirth is used not only for the benefits to the baby, but also to remind women of their original sin. It is another form of patriarchal control.

Examination

It is vital to know the key scenes in a text. Birth Day is a key section in the novel. Explore the variety of debates posed in this section.

Chapter 20

In the master bedroom Offred thinks of the struggles her mother's generation endured to give Offred's generation more freedom and equality.

The Handmaids were told that the 'slogan' that they recited three times every

day after their meal, '*From each*, says the slogan, *according to her ability; to each according to his needs*', came from the New Testament. Offred does not recognise the original source, which is from Karl Marx's critique of capitalism. Not only is the statement itself distorted, it is fraudulently presented as biblical authority. This is yet another example of how language

Language

is distorted in the Republic.

'You are a transitional generation, said Aunt Lydia. It is the hardest for you. We know the sacrifices you are being expected to make.'

Atwood cleverly juxtaposes this statement ahead of Offred's memory of the

film of her mother in a feminist pro-abortion demonstration in the early 1970s. Offred's mother was a typical feminist of that time, who fought for abortion, the equal rights amendment and against pornography. She was a single mother in a time when this was morally frowned upon. Some feminists were so against the traditional female roles of wife and mother that they criticised her for desiring motherhood.

Women and feminism

Many of these women forswore motherhood. These are the Unwomen of Gilead who are sent to the Colonies to clean up the toxic waste. Luke liked to tease Offred's mother about her convictions, and she would get upset when Offred said that she was getting worked up over nothing.

Like Offred's transitional generation of Handmaids, Offred's mother was part of a transitional generation of women. Throughout this section, Atwood presents the complex issues concerning feminism and anti-feminism that contributed to women's loss of freedom. Where do you think Atwood stands on the issue?

Coursework

Pay close attention to the arguments presented. Distinguish between the views of the characters and those of the author. See Question 2, page 63.

Chapter 21

Ofwarren gives birth.

The panting and chanting of the Handmaids during the birth recalls Janine's torment at the Red Centre in Chapter 13. This foreshadows the tragedy of

Ofwarren's baby being declared an Unbaby. She is a victim throughout her life.

Social, historical context

The birthing stool was used by the New England Puritans, and has been resurrected in Gilead for natural childbirth. The birthing stool positions are reminiscent of the position of the Handmaid and the Commander's Wife during the Ceremony, with the Wife in a higher position behind, or above, the Handmaid depending on one's perspective.

Offred has a conversation in her head with her mother: 'You wanted a women's culture. Well, now there is one. It isn't what you meant, but it exists. Be thankful for small mercies.' Explain what Offred's mother meant by a 'women's culture', and how this term has been misinterpreted by the Patriarchs of Gilead.

Coursework

Compare the various women's relationships presented in this section: between the Handmaids, between the Wives, and between the Wives and the Handmaids.

See Question 2, page 63.

Chapter 22

In her room, exhausted after the birth, Offred is too tired to tell her own story. Instead she recounts the story of Moira's successful escape from the Red Centre.

In this chapter Offred directly addresses the audience for the first time: 'I'm too tired to go with this story. I'm too tired to think about where I am. Here is a different story, a better one. This is the story of what happened to Moira.' Why does she do this? Gradually Atwood is preparing us for the revelation in the Historical Notes that Offred is telling her story into a tape recorder.

Narrative technique

The narrative technique in this chapter is complicated. Offred tells us a story of Moira's escape within the story of Janine's conversation with Aunt Lydia. How does this narrative technique lend itself to humour?

In terms of narrative structure, this chapter is linked with the story of Moira's first attempted escape in Chapter 15. Moira's failed attempt echoes Offred's family's unsuccessful escape. Subtly our expectations are being raised as to whether Offred will successfully flee from Gilead. In fact, Offred only thinks of Moira's escape after repressing the memory of how she came to be trapped inside the regime. 'That's how tired I am: as when you'd driven all night, into the dawn, for some reason, I won't think about that now, keeping each other awake with stories and taking turns at the wheel ...'

The narrative also invites a sharp contrast between instances of resistance and conformity. Moira is a character foil to Janine. Moira's strength, courage, unconventionality and independence serve to make Janine all the more pathetic and helpless by comparison. Where does Offred stand?

'She was now a loose woman.'

The Handmaids are both in awe of and frightened by Moira's escape. Moira

is both on the loose and set loose from being a Handmaid. It is Moira's will to be free that they find threatening because 'Already we were losing the taste for freedom…'.

In an utopian society freedom is crucial to fulfilling the needs of the individual. Only dysfunctional societies foster no desire for freedom. Freedom allows individuals to realise their potential and contribute to society. A society characterised by

Dystopian literature

a lack of desire for freedom, is a society in which people are more concerned with being protected than with being an individual. Ironically the Handmaids have a great deal of freedom. The freedom upon which they have become dependent is freedom from, or, more precisely, protection.

Gilead is riddled with practical flaws. The Aunts have not yet ironed all of the wrinkles out of their system at the Red Centre. Gileadean law, forbidding the Angels to look at women, assists Moira in her escape. The Angels do not have a good idea of what Aunt Elizabeth looks like, nor do they pay attention to her pass.

Chapter 23

Offred has her first secret meeting with the Commander.

Offred's confusing opening narrative anticipates her first clandestine meeting

with the Commander. Are her comments being made before the meeting, or in retrospect before 'reconstructing' the meeting? She contemplates the powers of forgiveness and oppression. The Commander represents the class in Gilead that holds the power to oppress women. At the same time,

Offred

she is aware of her own power to forgive him as an individual. During their meeting she also considers the power of being desired, 'to want is to have a weakness' and of physical force, 'I think about the blood coming out of him, hot as soup, sexual, over my hands.' His request for her to kiss him, 'as if you mean it', makes her realise that he is just as isolated and lonely as she is. Offred is aware that the balance of power in their relationship goes two ways. Will she forgive him?

At first Offred feels like a subservient little girl when she enters the Commander's office. The Scrabble game empowers her. Ironically, it is these voyages into 'the time before' in the Commander's office that fuel Offred's desire for freedom. Why are the last two chapters included in the section 'Birth Day'?

'Larynx, I spell. *Valance. Quince. Zygote.'*

Language

At first it is humorous that the Commander merely wished to play Scrabble with Offred, given that behind his closed doors he could have demanded anything of her. On closer consideration, however, it is apparent that the Scrabble game is inherently dangerous. In a society where reading and writing are activities permitted only to the elite, the Commander is flouting dogma by playing a word game with his Handmaid. The added element of risk makes the meeting all the more compelling. How do the words Offred spells communicate her feelings about being a Handmaid?

Examination

Up until this chapter we have only glimpsed the Commander in his official capacity. Offred's relationship with him is a key relationship in the text. Follow the development of this relationship and all other relationships presented. See Question 1, page 66.

■ Self-test questions Chapters 13–23

Who? What? Why? When? Where? How?

1 Where do Moira and Offred meet to talk?
2 Why are five members of the Quakers arrested?
3 What are the Commander's many personas during the prayers?
4 Where does Serena Joy sit during the Ceremony?
5 What does Offred wish she could steal from the kitchen?
6 Who does Offred think might have taken Luke in if he escaped to Canada?
7 When did schools start shutting down?
8 What are the films about that were shown at the Red Centre?
9 How do the other Handmaids learn of Moira's escape?
10 What words does Offred spell during the Scrabble game?

Prove it

Provide textual evidence for the following statements.

1 Janine adopts the ideology of Gilead wholeheartedly.
2 There are many signs of hope in Chapter 14.
3 The Handmaids are valued only as wombs.
4 Serena Joy hates the Ceremony.
5 Offred hopes to be reunited with Luke in the future.
6 There is rivalry between the women.
7 Offred's generation took their freedom and equality for granted.
8 Gileadean sexual ethics assisted Moira in her escape from the Red Centre.
9 Offred feels sorry for the Commander.
10 Only women are forbidden from reading in Gilead.

What is the significance?

Identify the speaker, the context of the passage and its significance.

1 'I feel my shoe soften, blood flows into it, it grows warm, it becomes a skin.'

2 'Then comes the mouldy old Rachel and Leah stuff we had drummed into us at the Centre.'

3 'It is an incendiary device: who knows what we'd make of it, if we ever got our hands on it?'

4 'But would I like his white, tufted raw body any better?'

5 'I want Luke here so badly. I want to be held and told my name.'

6 'I am like a room where things once happened and now nothing does, except the pollen of the weeds that grow up outside the window, blowing in as dust across the floor.'

7 'History will absolve me.'

8 'at my own high school thousands of years before ...'

9 'Moira is a loose woman.'

10 'They would taste also of lime. The letter C. Crisp, slightly acid on the tongue, delicious.'

Part IX Night

Chapter 24

Offred contemplates her new relationship with the Commander and laughs herself to sleep in her cupboard.

While Offred's changed relationship with the Commander seems to empower her, and makes her life in Gilead more tolerable, there are also strong signs of warning in this chapter.

'All this she would have believed, because otherwise how could she have kept on living?'

Imagery and motifs

Firstly, Offred recalls that the mistress of a Nazi war criminal, who protested at him being called a monster during a documentary forty or fifty years after the war, killed herself shortly thereafter. Then, after a fit of hysteria leads Offred to her cupboard, she reads the message of her predecessor. Offred is still ignorant of the former Offred's fate. We learn in Chapter 45 that the previous Offred was involved in the same special relationship with the Commander, but was discovered by Serena Joy. She hung herself from the chandelier rather than face public execution. The message is a warning to Offred not to make the same mistake.

'All I can hear now is the sound of my own heart, opening and closing, opening and closing, opening'

On the surface Offred is falling asleep. Symbolically she is being transformed, emotionally, by her heart opening itself to the Commander and then closing itself off again. Not only does the closing word of the chapter indicate the direction of her emotional transformation, it also prepares us for a new opening in Offred's situation. Pay close attention to the change in tone and language in Offred's narrative during the next section.

Why is the imagery of her suffering from hysteria appropriate?

Examination

Consider the placement of this memory of the Nazi mistress. Why is it placed here in the narrative? Why did the woman kill herself? Why does Offred remember the makeup?

See Question 1, page 66.

Part X Soul Scrolls

Chapter 25

Offred enjoys the height of summer because of the ripeness of Serena Joy's garden and the glimpses of normality during her meetings with the Commander.

Offred's awakened femininity is reflected in her sensitivity to, and enjoyment

Imagery and motifs

of, the colours and scents of Serena Joy's garden. The beauty of the garden even reminds Offred of poetry, another medium of romance. The garden's natural fruitfulness is a reproach to Serena Joy, much like Offred herself. The sexual imagery of the flowers reflects Offred's new role of mistress, and unofficial rival of the Wife.

Imagery of life and death is also evident throughout the chapter. Cora thinks that Offred is dead at the beginning of the chapter. Ironically, Offred has never felt so alive in Gilead. Look at the vitality of the language used to describe Serena's garden: 'The summer dress rustles against the flesh of my thighs, the grass grows underfoot, at the edges of my eyes there are movements, in the branches; feathers, flittings, grace notes, tree into bird, metamorphosis run wild.'

Despite Offred's insouciance, tension is created in the thread of narrative having to do with illness. For the Wives, illness can be a mere social pretence. For Handmaids and Marthas, illness can be fatal. This imagery serves as a reminder that Gilead is an environmentally and politically diseased society. The effect of the contrast between the imagery of creativity and disease is to maintain tension within the narrative. Offred's happiness will be short-lived.

Chapter 26

The next Ceremony is performed. It is a different experience for both the Commander and Offred.

The narrative of Offred's life in the Commander's home from Chapters 2 to 25 took place over four days. Keep track of the events of those days. Now the narrative has speeded up. In the last two chapters we have moved from the May to June. The succession in the previous chapter of Offred's nights with the Commander creates a feeling that time is passing quickly. The pace of the narrative is changing to add variety and tension. It is appropriate that the narrative moved more slowly in the beginning to allow the situation to be established, and for background information to be conveyed.

So far there have been no flashbacks in this section. The lack of flashbacks reinforces Offred's improved feelings of self worth.

Offred's improved self esteem is also emphasised in the way she speaks to the Commander: 'You can see from the way I was speaking to him that we were already on different terms.' She reproaches him for touching her during the Ceremony. How has Offred's changing relationship with the Commander been evident in her exchanges with him? How is Offred's life becoming more familiar to our experience?

'To him I am not merely empty.'

Offred now identifies herself as the Commander's mistress. She does not feel

Offred

as lonely, isolated or inferior as she did earlier in her narrative. In one sense she is still empty, in that she has yet to conceive. However, in two senses she is not merely empty to the Commander. Firstly she is no longer a nonentity – he knows her as an individual, and is gaining more insight into the reality of the Handmaid's existence. Secondly, she is more than just an empty womb to him; she is his mistress.

Some of the dangers Offred was symbolically warned about in Chapter 24 are coming to the fore. She has to be especially careful not to give anything away in front of Serena Joy during the Ceremony.

Chapter 27

Ofglen informs Offred that there is a resistance movement.

'hope is rising in me, like sap in a tree.'

Offred's hope is boosted when she learns of the resistance movement. Note

Offred

that when the Handmaids finally discover that they are like-minded, their conversation is reminiscent of Offred's joking with Moira. This note of hope is, however, undermined by a sinister tone throughout the chapter. The Eyes' brutality against the man with the briefcase reminds Offred that she is in perpetual danger. Which laws has she broken?

Chapter 28

Offred cannot sleep during her nap. Instead she recalls the events leading up to the formation of the Republic.

Social, historical context

This chapter, together with the previous chapter, provides background information on various societal and environmental conditions which led to the coup d'état on the American government.

We learned in the previous chapter that whales are extinct, and possibly many other species of fish and sea life. Fresh seafood is no longer available due to over-fishing. The other factors that led to the decline and fall of the American way of life were relaxed attitudes towards marriage and sex, centrally controlled technologies, sexual perversion, a drop in the birth rate and militant feminism. How are both Moira and Offred guilty of immorality with regard to sexual relationships? Why would it have been more difficult for the fundamentalists to take over if there had still been portable money? Look back at Chapters 4 and 11 for references to government controlled data. What areas of an individual's life does the government monitor?

Offred describes the transition phase between her old way of life and becoming a Handmaid. Most events happened very rapidly, such as women being banned from the workplace, women losing the right to own property, and the presence of armed guards at Offred's workplace. There were, nonetheless, signs beforehand that freedom was vanishing immediately after the military take-over. The newspapers had either been shut down or censored, which would have had the immediate impact of keeping society at large ignorant of certain current events, and of the truth of others. There were roadblocks and Identipasses. There was also the menacing sign that older women seemed to be disappearing.

Examination

This section provides much background information. There was no one single cause for the downfall of the USA and the formation of the Republic. List all of the factors that contributed to the creation of Gilead.

Narrative technique

Pay attention to the subtle narrative pattern of the chapter based around judgement. Offred begins the chapter by wondering what Moira would think of her relationship with the Commander. She naturally draws parallels with Moira's disapproval of her relationship with Luke. It is this line of thought that leads on to her memory of the coup d'état. She returns to the present longing to tell her mother that she no longer judges her so harshly. Back in the present she wonders how Nick judges her, and hopes that she is right to think well of him. Her doubts about Nick recall her doubts about Luke during the transition phase.

Notice, too, that in these last two chapters Offred has told part of her narrative in flashbacks again, whereas Chapters 25 and 26 contained no memories of the time before.

Chapter 29

That evening Offred asks the Commander about her predecessor, and demands to know the truth about Gilead.

'The pen between my fingers is sensuous, alive almost, I can feel its power, the power of the words it contains.'

Offred's freedoms during her clandestine meetings with the Commander afford her the opportunity to revel in the power of language. We witnessed in Chapter 26 how her use of verbal language towards the Commander had changed. This chapter opens with a description of how her body language has changed: 'I no longer sit stiff-necked, straight-backed, feet regimented side by side on the floor, eyes at the salute. Instead my body's lax, cosy even.' She also enjoys the luxury of reading. She has read a range of material from gossipy magazines to literature. The Commander finds her craving for reading sexually stimulating. This particular evening she deviates from written to spoken communication. Her present life forbids all forms of written language, and permits minimal oral communication. Through her enquiries about her predecessor, she makes two important discoveries. She learns that she is not the first Handmaid to enjoy such freedoms with the Commander. She also realises that her life is in his hands, and this gives her a new power over him in terms of his guilt if he were responsible for her death.

The description of Offred writing is sexually explicit. 'Pen Is Envy' is a play on the Freudian theory of 'Penis Envy'. This theory postulated that women envy men their penis because it is an external sex organ. Its visibility makes it a more powerful symbol of sexual power than a hidden vagina. Offred envies the Commander's freedom to have a pen. The pen has become a symbol of sexual power on two levels. Firstly pens are now solely associated with the elite male power base. Secondly the pen is a medium through which ideas can be represented. How does Offred suggest the creative force of the penis in her description of the feel of the pen?

Most of the language Offred has access to is distorted. Language shapes reality. Offred demands to know the truth about Gilead, rather than the distortions she has learned from the Red Centre and from her monthly glimpses of the news.

So far Offred has not had any flashbacks to her previous life when in the Commander's office. One purpose her memories serve is to exercise her language facilities. Her memories are a dialogue with herself where she explores ideas. She has no need to do this when in the Commander's Office because she is engaged in language practice while she is there.

Part XI Night

Chapter 30

Offred's memories of Luke and her daughter are fading. She prays to God to give her the will to survive.

Imagery and motifs

The image of falling permeates this chapter. Firstly night has fallen. The longing look between Nick and Offred indicates that they are falling in love. Offred is falling into spiritual darkness because her memories of Luke and her daughter are falling away from her; they are losing solidity and becoming ghosts. Offred uses supernatural imagery in the paragraph about her fading memories: 'I try to conjure, to raise my own spirits, from wherever they are.' In her version of the Lord's prayer she refers to Adam and Eve's fall from the grace. She acknowledges that knowledge is a temptation and that the original fall was 'a fall from innocence to knowledge.'

Part XII Jezebel's

Chapter 31

Offred learns more about the resistance movement. Serena Joy devises a plan to help Offred conceive.

Social, historical context

Jezebel was the wife of King Ahab in I Kings. She brought wickedness upon his kingdom. Puritans used the name Jezebel to label dissenting women in their townships. This section focuses on dissenting women in Gilead. Ofglen is dissenting through her membership in the Mayday resistance movement. Ofglen and Offred indulge in conversations through their 'amputated speech'. Serena Joy tells Offred that Gilead is rife with acts of dissension in order to produce babies.

There are also religious dissenters. These men and women are 'salvaged' and hung on the Wall. There are obvious parallels here between Gilead's treatment of religious dissenters and periods of history in other societies when religious dissenters were persecuted and killed.

Many of the Commanders are sterile. Towards the end of the twentieth century the sperm counts had fallen for a variety of reasons. The Commanders belong to this generation of affected men.

July the fourth was referred to as Independence Day because it marked the beginning of America as an independent country. Why have they stopped celebrating this holiday in Gilead? Labour Day was a holiday for workers on the first Monday of September. What do you think the holiday celebrates in Gilead?

Chapter 32

Offred lies on her bed and thinks about the Commander's justification for the creation of the Republic.

'This lack of fear was dangerous.'

Although she seems to be enjoying privileges from everyone at present,

Offred is always aware of her precarious situation. Instead of smoking the cigarette, she saves the match in case of emergency.

Offred's relish of the Commander's alcohol-tasting kisses foreshadows their trip to the Jezebel's night-club. She learns that the puritanical practices were resurrected to make men feel more for women. The men who made the decision were

Offred

conscious of the suffering women would endure. Back in her room after her rendezvous with the Commander, the air is heavy and still and she feels buried alive. She foresees her own end in identification with her predecessor.

Chapter 33

Offred attends a Prayvaganza and learns that Janine's baby was declared an Unbaby.

Tension is building in this section. Increasingly there seems to be no way out of a Handmaid's existence. Learning of Janine's deformed baby, Offred is reminded that becoming pregnant does not guarantee a Handmaid's survival. Remembering Janine's nervous breakdown at the Red Centre also reminds Offred of what happens to the weak in Gilead. It also reminds her of Moira's escape, which foreshadows Offred's encounter with Moira at

Offred

Jezebel's.

Chapter 34

Twenty Angels get married to twenty Daughters at the Prayvaganza.

'Arranged marriages have always worked out just as well, if not better.'

Many people today would agree with the Commander's comment. Traditionally marriages were arranged in order to secure land, power, political

Women and feminism

or social status, or a combination of the three. In many cultures arranged marriages still take place. Supporters of arranged marriages argue that because the marriage is based on something tangible, the marriage is more successful than a marriage determined by love, which is intangible. There are advantages and drawbacks to both arranged and non-arranged marriages. Think of these in relation to both sexes. To Offred, an arranged marriage denies the experience of falling in love, thus reinforcing her romantic nature. Her insistence on falling in love anticipates her intimate relationship with Nick, although their initial meeting is arranged. How do you reconcile the Commander's views on the advantages of arranged marriages with his secret meetings with Offred? He may not be falling in love with her, but is the intimacy more than merely improving his chances of a successful conception?

No women in Gilead are valued as equal with men. At the marriage ceremony the privileged Daughters of the Commanders have to plead subservience to their husbands: 'But I suffer not a woman to teach, nor to usurp authority over the man, but to be in silence.' The biblical authority used in the ceremony is from I Timothy 2:9–15.

Chapter 35

Serena Joy brings Offred a photograph of her daughter.

> **'An invalid, one who has been invalidated. No valid passport. No exit.'**

This entire chapter is about Offred's feelings of being invalidated in her present life. She cannot leave Gilead physically or through suicide. She fears

Offred

she will never have the opportunity to fall in love again, because that, too, has been invalidated by the regime. The photograph of her daughter deepens her feelings for she knows that evidence of Handmaids will be erased from Gilead, and she fears that she has already been erased from her daughter's memory. Offred's memories no longer strengthen her resolve to survive. Throughout the narrative Offred has experienced opposing emotions towards love and death, survival and suicide.

Examination

Characters are developed in novels. Record how Offred changes over the course of the novel. To what extent is she a believable character?

Chapter 36

The Commander surprises Offred with a night out.

'Up for a little excitement?'

Ever since his private meetings with Offred began, the Commander has been

Dystopian literature

breaking the Gileadean rules. Firstly, he is not supposed to meet with her apart from at the official Ceremony. Secondly, he allows her to read material he has procured from the black market. Now he goes one step further and takes her out in provocative attire. Despite any disobedience, the Commander wanted the Republic, and supports the Gileadean marriage and Handmaid practices. As a Commander of the new regime,

he should be a model member of society. In fact the society was created to suit him and his peers. The society is failing if its leaders, the very people whom it benefits, find its laws too restrictive.

Chapter 37

Jezebel's night-club. Offred spots Moira.

'Nature demands variety, for men.'

This government-run brothel is another means by which the elite male sector

Women and feminism

uses women in Gilead. Handmaids are used for procreation. The prostitutes are used purely for sex. How does Offred feel about seeing the other women? The foreign men remind her of how women are still treated outside of Gilead. Which is more demeaning for women, being Handmaids or prostitutes at a brothel?

Chapter 38

Moira tells Offred the story of her escape and post-Red Centre Life.

Narrative technique

Atwood has been preparing us for the reappearance of Moira. On the way to the club, Offred thinks of Moira twice. In terms of the narrative it is logical that Moira reappears at this point. Moira's nonconformist attitude and her heroic escape from the Red Centre have been a talisman to Offred. Moira needs to reappear now to tell the rest of her story after her escape.

We are also being prepared for the end of Offred's story. First the mystery of what happened to Moira is resolved through their reacquaintance at Jezebel's. Secondly, we will learn why her other talisman, her predecessor, committed suicide (because Serena Joy learned of her outing to none other than Jezebel's). Ultimately we are being prepared for Offred's escape from Gilead. Unlike her predecessor, Offred is taken away in a black van, and presumably follows the Underground Femaleroad.

Through Moira's narrative, a second mystery is solved: what happens in the Colonies. Moira's description of the Colonies enlightens us about this possibility for Offred. The narrative style switches halfway through the chapter from the present to a future time when Offred is recounting Moira's story. Why is this switch necessary? What is the effect of her closing statement?

Social, historical context

The Underground Femaleroad is based on the Underground Railroad, which helped 30,000 slaves to freedom in Canada before the abolition of slavery in America in 1864. Like the Underground Femaleroad, the Underground Railroad was a series of homes of supporters of the cause. Slaves would be secretly transferred from home to home until they were safely over the Canadian border. Many parallels can be drawn between the treatment of women in Gilead and the historical treatment of blacks in America.

We discover why Offred and her family had to escape Gilead, in spite of the fact that they were a family unit: 'As long as you said you were some sort of a Christian and you were married, for the first time that is, they were still leaving you pretty much alone.' This was Luke's second marriage, which invalidated them as suitable parents under the new regime.

> **'The other Colonies are worse, though, the toxic dumps and the radiation spills.'**

More details are provided about the environmental issues that contributed to the formation of Gilead. The Colonies are populated by older women, unsuccessful Handmaids and gay men, thereby reinforcing the idea that people are only valued for their reproductive possibilities.

Chapter 39

The Commander takes Offred to a hotel room to attempt old-fashioned sex.

Offred cannot respond to the Commander for many reasons. She is a romantic

Offred

and cannot, therefore, respond to the Commander because she is not in love with him. This situation is made worse by the fact that this particular hotel holds memories of Luke. The Commander does himself no favours, either, when he strokes her ankle. Her tattoo reminds her that she is his property, a mere national resource. The tattoo is also a symbol that she is a prisoner of his regime. Finally, her personal feelings towards the Commander are becoming less sympathetic. Why is the story about Offred's mother included as a separate narrative in this chapter rather than the preceding one? How does her language indicate her change of attitude?

Self-test questions Chapters 24–39

Who? What? Why? When? Where? How?
1 How old is Offred?
2 How many more chances does she have to produce a baby?
3 What are Soul Scrolls?
4 Who is blamed for the coup d'état?
5 What holiday is celebrated in Gilead?
6 Why were the Jewish given a choice to leave Gilead?
7 Where does Offred recognise that she has been before?
8 How long was Moira underground?
9 What happened to Offred's mother?
10 Why didn't Luke want Offred to ring the police after they visited her mother's apartment?

Prove it
Provide textual evidence for the following statements.
1 The Commander is ignorant of the true conditions under which Handmaids live.
2 Offred's predecessor met secretly with the Commander in his office.
3 The Commander is ruthless underneath his gentle exterior.
4 Getting pregnant is no guarantee of security for a Handmaid's life.
5 No women in Gilead are valued as equal to men.
6 Offred cares about Nick's opinion of her.
7 Women are still debased in Gilead.
8 Moira was tortured after her capture on the Underground Femaleroad.
9 The trip to Jezebel's and meeting with Moira change Offred's attitude towards the Commander.
10 Offred's memory is being affected by her lack of opportunity to read or write.

What is the significance?
Identify the speaker, the context of the passage and its significance.
1 'Partly I was jealous of her; but how could I be jealous of a woman so obviously dried-up and unhappy?'
2 'There are five different prayers: for health, wealth, a death, a birth, a sin.'
3 'The Book of Job.'
4 'Context is all; or is it ripeness?'
5 'Oh God, King of the universe, thank you for not creating me a man.'
6 'Aunt Lydia sucks.'
7 'Who are these people?'
8 'They like to see you all painted up. Just another crummy power trip.'
9 'She is frightening me now, because what I hear in her voice is indifference, a lack of volition.'
10 'She might as well be [dead], said Moira. You should wish it for her.'

Part XIII Night

Chapter 40

Later the same night, after returning from Jezebel's, Offred begins her love affair with Nick.

Narrative technique

The thunderstorm brewing in Chapter 32 is about to release its electrical build-up and rain. Similar to the thunderstorm building up electricity, Offred has been building up powerful emotions that need to be released. This has been Offred's most eventful day in the novel. She has contemplated the absence of love in Gilead, the alternatives for women within the regime should she fail to conceive, and the ruthless power her Commander represents. One of her sources of strength, the heroic ideal of Moira's escape, has been exposed as flawed. She has, moreover, had to face the reality of being forgotten by her daughter and of her mother's fate in the Colonies. Had the final episode of the night not occurred, she would have been understandably suicidal. It seems she has little reason to survive. The one redeeming force she had not anticipated, love, saves her in her darkest hour.

Although neither version of her first encounter with Nick is factually accurate, the feelings presented are real. Both versions reveal Offred releasing her pent-up anger, fear, loneliness and desire. Look closely at each version. How do they differ? What emotions are emphasised in each?

Note the placing of this chapter. It directly follows the Commander's pathetic attempt to have sex with Offred. This structure serves to emphasise the contrast between the two experiences for Offred. Compare the language and tone used in each. Why does she only think she is betraying Luke when she is with Nick, not the Commander?

Examination

Juxtaposition is used skilfully throughout the novel to emphasise meanings. Identify all the instances of juxtaposition and the meaning highlighted.

Part XIV Salvaging

Chapter 41

Narrative technique

The transformation of Offred's life is communicated immediately in her change of tone. The narrative has become more feminine in that it is emotive, not factual. She is no longer cynical or longing, but apologetic and self-conscious. Suspense is also built up as we wonder what she is so ashamed to tell us.

Offred's apology is an interesting comment on the nature of memory: 'I'm sorry it's in fragments, like a body caught in crossfire or pulled apart by force.' Through Offred's apology and direct address to the audience, Atwood is preparing us for the revelation in Historical Notes of the true source of her narrative.

'The fact is that I no longer want to leave, escape, cross the border to freedom.'

Up to this chapter, Offred has been a shrewd observer of the world around her. Her perspective has altered dramatically in this chapter. Being in love has made her selfish, and this comes through in her narrative. She can adjust to living within the confines of the regime because she has now achieved what she missed most: love.

Imagery and motifs

Which words make the following description of Nick erotic? 'I want to see what can be seen, of him, take him in, memorise him, save him up so I can live on the image, later: the lines of his body, the texture of his flesh, the glisten of sweat on his pelt, his long sardonic unrevealing face.' Compare this description to the description of the Commander's naked body in Chapter 39. How does the precariousness of Offred's relationship with Nick make the scene even more thrilling? What other images dominate the chapter?

Note how excitement, tension and suspense are building in this section as we approach the climax of the novel.

See Question 1, page 62.

Coursework

Chapter 42

Offred attends a Women's Salvaging.

Imagery and motifs

Offred describes the Salvaging as if it is Commencement: 'I think of hats, pastel hats worn by some of the mothers, and of the black gowns the students would put on, and the red ones.' (Commencement is the graduation ceremony at an American University.) Ironically, much of the radical thinking which Gilead reviles emanated from university campuses.

Dystopian literature

That Salvagings have spawned copycat crimes is an embarrassment to the Gileadean government. It seems that these public executions for named crimes have the opposite effect from the one intended. They serve to give the Handmaids more resolve to fight the system and ideas of how to do this, hence, the crimes of the women are no longer revealed. There are still many wrinkles that need ironing out of the system in Gilead. We will learn of more changes of policy in the Historical Notes.

'It's hard to believe there will not be polite clapping after this speech, and tea and cookies served on the lawn.'

The solemn and sober authority of these occasions is further subverted by Offred's cynical tone.

Chapter 43

The Particicution.

Gileadean practice does not honour the Commandment 'Thou shalt not kill.'

Dystopian literature

Throughout the novel many examples of legalised killing have occurred. The term Particicution is an amalgamation of participation and execution. Crowds can either be a force of good, providing protection through anonymity, or a force of evil, exploiting the brute strength of numbers. The strong feelings manipulated out of the Handmaids create mass hysteria. Atwood demonstrates the danger of mob mentality; a victory of emotion over rationality.

Janine's drift into madness suggests that true converts are driven insane by the society's inhumanity. The cultural practices are not a civilising force, but a brutalising one. In contrast, Ofglen's act of mercy serves to highlight the remnants of humanity alive in the resistance movement. Why is this is the most disturbing chapter in the novel?

Chapter 44

By afternoon, Ofglen has committed suicide rather than betray the resistance movement. She is replaced by a treacherous new Ofglen.

'Now that Ofglen is gone I am alert again, my sluggishness has fallen away, my body is no longer for pleasure only but senses its jeopardy.'

Ofglen's disappearance jolts Offred back to reality. Ironically, she takes her

Offred

greatest risk in trying the Mayday password when she has regained her senses. She realises the extent of the danger she has immersed herself in through forming relationships with others. Paradoxically, it is because of her relationships that she must know what happened to Ofglen, out of regard for the other Handmaid and also out of fear for herself and her loved ones. In the face of Ofglen's heroism, Offred confronts her cowardice. Compare the two Handmaids.

Chapter 45

Offred's relationship with the Commander is discovered by Serena Joy.

Language

The appropriate use of allusion contributes to the rising interest of the chapter.

'She has died that I may live' is a variation of the Christian doctrine centred on the meaning of Christ's crucifixion: 'He died that we may live.' Offred changes the semantics to make the avowal feminine and personal. The parallel also invites us to see Ofglen as a Christ figure.

'I don't want to be a dancer ...' is an allusion to the 1948 film *The Red Shoes*, in which a ballerina dances herself to death. What is its significance here?

'I feel, for the first time, their true power' is an allusion to the end of George Orwell's dystopian novel *Nineteen Eighty-four*. In Orwell's novel the protagonist, Winston Smith, in a broken state, finally accepts the totalitarian regime 'The Brotherhood'. Unlike Winston, we never learn Offred's fate. Also unlike Winston, her resignation to the power under which she lives, comes about not as the result of physical torture, but through her guilt at being a coward.

This chapter is characterised by a feeling of emotional distance. How does the language create this effect?

Coursework

Atwood borrows from many genres in this novel. What elements of the romance genre are evident in this chapter?

Part XV Night

Chapter 46

The black van comes for Offred, but it turns out to be the Mayday resistance movement.

Many earlier ideas are wound together in the chapter. As Offred waits, her

Imagery and motifs

options of what she could do are echoes of failed survival. In turn she recalls Moira, Ofglen and her predecessor. She is once again waiting. She notices that night has fallen more quickly. Summer is ending and nights are getting longer, but the comment also reminds us that the events of the preceding four chapters have taken place just that day. So much has happened to shatter her existence that she had not noticed the time pass.

Offred remarks that, 'There were always two of us.' The image of doubles has run throughout the narrative. Go back and note all of the references to doubles.

Offred's narrative closes with poetic symbolism: 'And so I step up, into the darkness within; or else the light.' She is either going to her death, or her freedom. To reassure Offred, Nick calls her by real name. It serves as a password, much like the resistance's code word, Mayday.

As she is accompanied out of the Commander's house, she is aware of her betrayal of her position. Why does the Commander look 'worried and helpless'? Her betrayal of the Commander with 'Violation of state secrets' provides a clue to the identity of her Commander in the Historical Notes.

Offred

Historical Notes on The Handmaid's Tale

Two hundred years later, Offred's account of her life under the Gileadean regime is the subject of a symposium on Gileadean Studies.

Examiners often ask candidates to evaluate the contribution of additional material at the end of a text.

See Question 2, page 66.

Examination

Social, historical context

Although this epilogue is set two hundred years in the future, the occasion of a university symposium and the details of upcoming activities for the participants in Nunavit, are more familiar to us than the details of Gileadean life. There are, however, many subtle diversions from our experience as well. Firstly, the culture presented in the future is characterised by non-Caucasian cultures studying Caucasian culture. Western academia has traditionally been characterised by Caucasians studying anthropology, eastern philosophy and eastern religions. Much of this section is a gentle mockery of current academic practice and language. Despite the advances in non-Caucasian academia, the male perspective of this particular paper is typical of the historical male dominance and perspective in academic research.

'The superscription "The Handmaid's Tale" was appended to it by Professor Wade, partly in homage to the great Geoffrey Chaucer ...'

Chaucer wrote *The Canterbury Tales*, between 1380 and 1400. There are only two female characters on the pilgrimage to Canterbury: a Prioress and a five-times married woman, the Wife of Bath who gives a rambling autobiographical prologue before her tale. Her prologue argues the importance of female experience over male authority. Like the Wife of Bath seven hundred years earlier, the significance of Offred's experience is invalidated by the power of male authority in 2195. Like the ruling class in Gilead, the Wife of Bath's fifth husband dominates her by distorting authoritative texts. The Wife of Bath remains identified in literary memory by her status as a wife. Offred, too, remains defined by her Commander.

This postscript to Offred's story indicates that societal conditions for women became worse and the regime even more severe in the Middle Gileadean period.

The historical glance back at Gilead, what preceded it and what was happening in other parts of the world at the same time, has the impact of drawing Offred's experience much closer in time to our own. It is unsettling and sobering to learn that Gileadean practices were based on real practices currently or formerly in existence: 'there was little that was truly original with or indigenous to Gilead: its genius was synthesis.' This serves to warn us that the reality of Gilead is not as far from our own experience as we thought while reading Offred's story. The function of any futuristic novel is to warn of possible consequences of contemporary trends. List all of the examples of real events that have contributed to the ideas presented in the narrative.

Narrative technique

The narrative technique in this section is different in terms of its form (dialogue) and language (academic and objective).

'all such arrangements are based on some guesswork and are to be regarded as approximate pending further research.'

Now that we know the reason for the fragmented quality of Offred's narrative, are there any segments that you would rearrange?

The Symposium ends with a request for questions, thereby inviting the reader to question the issues raised by Offred's narrative and the Historical Notes. Atwood's endings are often open-ended. What is gained by Offred's story not having a definitive ending?

Examination

Irony figures prominently in this section. Which details of Offred's account does Professor Pieixoto interpret incorrectly?

See Question 2, page 66.

Self-test questions Chapters 40–Historical Notes

Who? What? Why? When? Where? How?
1 Where is Nick's room?
2 What time of year is it?
3 When was the Salvaging announced?
4 Where are the Salvagings held?
5 How does the regime justify the Particicution?
6 Why does Offred want to go to the Wall with the new Ofglen?
7 How does Serena Joy discover Offred's affair with the Commander?
8 Who did Offred suspect of calling for the black van to take her away?
9 Where were the tapes discovered?
10 Where and when does the Twelfth Symposium on Gileadean Studies take place?

Prove it
Provide textual evidence for the following statements.
1 By the time she recounts her first night with Nick in Chapter 40, Offred has fallen in love with him.
2 She has regained her true identity through her relationship with Nick.
3 Nick replaces Luke in Offred's affections.
4 Offred cannot bear to watch the Salvaging.
5 Ofglen is courageous.
6 The new Ofglen is not part of the Mayday resistance movement.
7 Offred realises her own limits of courage in Chapter 45.
8 Suicide has always been an option for Offred.
9 Offred's Commander was probably Frederick R. Waterford.
10 Professor Pieixoto's paper misses the point of Offred's narrative.

What is the significance?
Identify the speaker, the context of the passage and its significance.
1 'Goodbye, I thought, even at the time, goodbye.'
2 'I tell, therefore you are.'
3 'I do not feel regret about this. I feel relief.'
4 'The bell is tolling ...'
5 'One of ours, I think. A Guardian. It seems impossible.'
6 'Things are back to normal.'
7 'Behind my back Nick has stopped whistling.'
8 'I have given myself over into the hands of strangers, because it can't be helped.'
9 'Denay, Nunavit.'
10 'He seems to have been the originator of the term "Particicution" ...'

◼ How to write a coursework essay

Different examining boards have different requirements for A Level coursework, but there are certain principles that hold good in every case. We will consider these and also two possible titles for coursework. However, essays can not only be of *different lengths*, but of different types. You are probably most likely to find yourself writing on one text (approximately 1,500–2,000 words), comparing two texts (3,000 words) or writing about a literary genre referring to at least three texts (up to 5,000 words). Most of these word–length requirements are optional maximums; *it is essential that you check with your teacher that there is no penalty for extra length.*

If you are choosing a comparative title, you must make sure that comparisons are made throughout, not necessarily in the same sentence, but at least in adjacent paragraphs. Your essay title must direct you to some specific comparison, not just a generalised survey of similarities and differences. Remember also that 'comparison' always implies 'contrast' as well: discussing different ways of approaching a theme, plot-line or genre can always be productive.

The single-text coursework essay is in many ways similar. A specific task is again essential, and once again your theme or line of argument must be kept before the reader throughout. Narration is almost always unhelpful: even at A Level, 'telling the story' is the most common failing. Almost equally dangerous is taking opinions from critics without fully understanding them and failing to absorb them into your arguments. *Copying* from critics without acknowledgement is, of course, plagiarism and can result in disqualification.

The need for a developing argument or comparison has implications for your method of approaching the essay. You should make general notes on the material (textual evidence, useful quotations, comments by critics, etc.), then shape them into an ordered framework (probably simply by numbering them in an appropriate order) before working through at least two or three drafts of the essay. You should be fully aware of what each paragraph is to be about, as far as possible signalling this to the reader in the first sentence, often called the *topic sentence* for this reason. With comparatively short essays like these, you should make sure that your style is concise and time is not wasted on unnecessary quotations. Relevant, fairly brief quotations are very valuable, absorbed into your sentences if very short, set out on separate lines if slightly longer. It is unlikely that quotations of more than a few lines will really help you.

The actual presentation of your essay is also important. With coursework it is sheer carelessness to make errors in spelling, punctuation or syntax or (worst of all) to confuse or misspell characters' names. Unless there is a definite reason for doing so, avoid slang and colloquialisms, including contractions like 'they've' for 'they have'.

The format of introduction-essay-conclusion is perfectly acceptable, but, used over-formally, can weight the essay too much in the direction of semi-relevant generalisation at the beginning and the end. In a good essay, the conclusion will simply be the final stage of a developed argument.

Each of the example titles given below can be easily adapted to a comparative essay with another text(s). Use the outlines to form your notes on this text. The points should also help you to focus your approach to the other text(s).

An *outline* of a model answer has been supplied for each essay title below. Use this outline in conjunction with material in the **Who's who**, **Themes, images and language** and **Text commentary** sections of this guide. In addition, the points raised as **Examiner's tips** throughout the **Text commentary** should prove particularly useful.

1 Discuss the variety of narrative techniques used in The Handmaid's Tale.

Approach this task by considering the following:

- The significance of the epigraphs.
- The ordering of the sections. How do the 'Night' sections contribute to the structure of the narrative? How are these sections different from the rest of the narrative?
- The deliberate confusion of the opening chapter.
- The fragmentation of the narrative.
- The use of flashbacks.
- The presentation of time. Explore the pacing of the narrative. How much time elapses during Offred's third placement? What is the total time span of the novel, including the Historical Notes?
- The variety of stories being told.
- The nature of storytelling explored in the text.
- Offred's dialogue with the audience.
- Balance within the narrative structure, both through characterisation and events.
- The contribution of the motifs of missing persons, ghosts and doubles to the structuring of the novel.
- The appropriateness of the open and ambiguous ending to Offred's narrative.

- The contrast between the style and perspective of Offred's tale and the Historical Notes.
- The variety of narrators.
- The variety of language used.

2 *Explore the issues concerning women and feminism raised in the novel.*

Approach this task by considering the following:
- The roles for women in Gilead.
- Women's status pre-Gilead.
- Women's status post-Gilead.
- The issue of women's freedom in pre-Gilead and Gilead.
- Women's relationships with other women.
- Women's relationships with men.
- The three generations of women in Offred's family.
- The presentation of motherhood: Offred's mother, Offred, Janine and Commander Warren's wife.
- Childbirth: natural versus medically assisted.
- The sisterhood of women: Gilead's view, Moira's view, Aunt Lydia's view and the author's view.
- The feminist movement. To what extent did it give rise to Gilead?
- A woman's culture.
- The author's stance on these issues.
- Female versus male perspectives in the narrative.

■ How to write an examination essay

Preparation

- The *first essential* is thorough revision. You may be answering questions in either a traditional examination or an Open Book examination. It is vital that you remember that in an Open Book examination you have enough time to look up quotations and references, but *only if you know where to look*.

- The revision process should begin well before the examination: a matter of months rather than weeks. Initially you need to re-read texts, which is not a good idea the week before the examination. It is then useful to make notes, both to assist memory at the time and to provide a summary for later revision. These notes should be arranged to give a pattern to your study: by themes, characters, techniques, etc. Quotations should not be learned simply by rote, but together with relevant uses for them. A late stage of revision should be to fix the patterns of knowledge in your mind, probably by writing practice essays.

- The time process is very important: trying to absorb new material the night before the examination is likely to be positively harmful.

Before you start writing

- Read the questions very carefully, both to choose the most suitable title and to be certain of exactly what you are asked to do. It is very easy, but potentially disastrous, to answer the essay you *hope or imagine* has been asked, or to reproduce the practice essay you wrote on a vaguely similar theme.

- A Level questions need careful attention. Do not respond instantly to a quotation without checking what the question asks you to write about it. Make certain that you are aware of every part of a question: many ask you to do two or three distinct things and omitting one of these immediately reduces your possible marks. Check words like compare, contrast, analyse, consider and discuss.

- You do not have much spare time in an examination, but it is worthwhile to spend a few minutes (ten, perhaps) noting down the material you think is relevant, matching it with the instructions you have been given and drawing up an essay plan. Starting on the wrong essay or starting the right one in the wrong way ultimately wastes time.

- Make sure that your plan develops a consistent argument or point of view: you will not be asked to tell the story, and essays that take a chronological approach seldom do well.

Writing the essay

- The first sentences are very important. You should begin the essay by informing the examiner of the opinion you are going to develop, the contrasts you are going to study or your view of the problem you are about to analyse. This should stay in focus throughout the essay: if possible, each paragraph should begin with a *topic sentence* relating the material of that paragraph to your overall theme or argument.

- Do not spend too long introducing the essay: move quickly to the material you wish to cover. Throughout, check your plan to make sure that you deal with all the points you wish to make.

- Quotation is particularly relevant where the style of expression is important in itself or in revealing character or the author's viewpoint. It is less important when you are referring to events. Quotations should be kept fairly short and should be relevant, not simply attractive or well-known. In many cases it is possible to absorb a quotation into your sentence, but quotations of a few lines must be set out separately and as in the text.

- There is no 'correct' length for an essay. The fact that someone else is clearly writing huge amounts does not mean that he/she will obtain better marks than you. However, you should make sure that you use your time fully, write concisely and avoid padding.

- It is dangerous to exceed the allotted time for each question by more than a few minutes, especially as marks can always be gained most easily at the start of an essay. Make sure that you tackle the required number of questions. For this reason, though an elegant conclusion is desirable, it may sometimes be necessary to omit it.

- Examiners understand that candidates are writing under pressure, but it is still important that you maintain as high a standard of written expression as possible. Avoid slang, colloquialisms and contractions (e.g. 'they've' for 'they have') wherever possible.

Examination questions inevitably invite the candidate to present an argument. Decide your position and make sure that you refer to both sides of the argument. Whether the question pertains to a theme or a specific scene in the text, you must demonstrate your knowledge of the whole text. Make sure that you refer to specific examples throughout the novel in your argument.

An *outline* of a model answer has been supplied for each essay title below. Use this outline in conjunction with material in the **Who's who**, **Themes, images and language** and **Text commentary** sections of this guide. In addition, the points raised as **Examiner's tips** throughout the Text commentary should prove particularly useful.

1 *Re-read Chapter 24 from 'I remember a television program I saw once;' to 'what I remember now, most of all, is the makeup.' Using this and other relevant references, respond to Atwood's presentation of the Commander in the novel.*

Approach this task by considering the following:

- The characterisation of the Commander is complex. He arouses both our fear and pity. Present both these responses to his character in your answer.
- The significance of this passage: Offred's new relationship with the Commander; the Commander's humanity and inhumanity; how history will judge the Commander's regime; Offred's reaction to this memory.
- The presentation of the Commander in his official capacity, Chapters 8, 15, and 16.
- His relationship with Serena Joy.
- The Commander's developing personal relationship with Offred, Chapters 25, 26 and 29.
- His attitude to the previous Offred, Chapter 29.
- His justification for the creation of Gilead, Chapter 32.
- His attitude to love, Chapter 34.
- His behaviour at Jezebel's, Chapters 36 and 37.
- Moira's story, Chapter 38.
- Offred's attitude to the Commander in the hotel room, Chapter 39.
- His appearance as Offred is escorted to the black van, Chapter 46.
- The information provided about the possible identities of Offred's Commander in the Historical Notes.

2 *To what extent are the Historical Notes necessary to the narrative of The Handmaid's Tale?*

Approach this task by considering the following:

- The significance of the location of the Twelfth Symposium.
- The importance of Professor Maryann Crescent Moon and what is revealed about the society of 2195 in her speech.
- The shift in the time setting of Gilead from the future to the past. How does placing Gilead in historical and cultural contexts affect the threat of such a regime?
- Which society is more similar to our own, Gilead or the society of 2195?
- The contrast in narrative style, tone and perspective between Offred's narrative and Professor Pieixoto's speech.

- What the Historical Notes add to our understanding of the narrative structure of the tale.
- The facts revealed about Gilead.
- How our view of the Commander is affected.
- Do the Notes affect the end of Offred's story?
- Professor Pieixoto's request for questions.
- The critique of historical methods.
- What would be lost, if anything, without the Historical Notes?

Self-test answers Chapters 1–12

Who? What? Why? When? Where? How?

1   The Commander's house is not her home. She has been assigned to live here and resists thinking of the bedroom as her room in her struggle to preserve her individual identity.
2   The Unwomen.
3   Five weeks.
4   The wives of the poorer men in Gilead.
5   Past the Wall to check for former loved ones.
6   Homosexuality.
7   Two years.
8   She has to choose between accepting the doctor's offer of an alternate way of becoming pregnant, thereby avoiding being declared Unwoman, and risking the death penalty for being caught.
9   Three years.
10 They are considered a national resource, and thereby property of the Republic of Gilead.

Prove it

1   In Chapter 4 she passes him on her way out shopping. She observes him closely, wonders how he might smell and sighs.
2   In Chapter 3 Offred tells us that the Wife in her previous posting spent most of her time in her room.
3   We are told in Chapter 5 that there are no more lawyers, and that the university is closed. Although there are still doctors, they do not live alongside the Commanders in the privileged 'heart' of Gilead. In Chapter 6 we are told that doctors and scientists are the victims of Men's Salvagings.
4   Walking past the hanging men, she feels relieved that Luke wasn't a doctor. She quickly corrects her verb tense to the present, 'Isn't'.
5   Offred mentions Moira's name in Chapter 1 as one of the names that was exchanged from bed to bed.
6   We have been given many details to this effect. The glass in the windows is shatterproof, the chandelier has been removed, along with anything else a rope could be tied to, and the mirror in the bathroom has been removed. A Martha has to wait outside the bathroom when a Handmaid bathes to ensure she does not drown herself. The Handmaids have committed suicide for a variety of reasons – some have been part of the Mayday resistance movement, and have taken their own lives, rather than have to inform on others when they have been found out. Others have not been able to cope with the situation, perhaps because the Commanders' Wives have made their lives a misery.
7   In Chapter 10 she says that, in the time before, 'We lived, as usual, by ignoring.' Her generation of women was able to dismiss stories about violence against women as irrelevant to their daily lives.
8   Moira and Offred's college dormitory used to be co-educational, but by the time they were there men and woman were segregated. There were also many cases of violence against women.
9   In Chapter 10 she thinks of the lyrics of Elvis Presley's 'Heartbreak Hotel'. The song is about frustration and loneliness. Later in the chapter she wishes she could spit or throw something out of the window at the Commander below to relieve her boredom and frustration. Given her active mind and lack of freedom, even to read or write, she must be unbearably frustrated.

10   Moira does not conform to conventions of appearance, thinking or behaviour while at college. She has one gold fingernail 'to be eccentric'; she wants to host an 'underwhore' party; and she leads Offred in dropping water bombs on boys below their dormitory window.

What is the significance?

1   Serena Joy, Chapter 3, to Offred during their first meeting. This passage indicates Serena Joy's possessiveness towards her husband.

2   Offred, Chapter 2, when describing the braided rug in the bedroom made by women. This society is a return to the traditional values of the Victorian era, such as the centrality of Christian religious teaching, sexual inequality, and racism.

3   Offred remembering one of Aunt Lydia's sayings as she passes through the heart of Gilead, Chapter 5. This saying is a distortion of the biblical passage, 'the kingdom of God is within you', which means that the opportunity to serve God lies within us. Aunt Lydia's distortion has two interpretations. It means that society takes precedence over the individual. It also reinforces the Handmaids' function, in that the future (generations) of Gilead is within their wombs.

4   Offred's reaction to the Japanese tourists' dress, Chapter 5. Offred finds the 'westernised' dress of the Japanese tourists exotic, although it is exactly the way she herself used to dress. The dress of the Japanese women is described in a sexually explicit way. Offred sees them from a man's point of view.

5   Offred on her bed during her memory trips to her former identity, Chapter 7. Offred highlights the fact that she is lying down. Lie is an intransitive verb, which means the action is not performed on anyone or anything. Lay is a transitive verb which requires an object. We can interpret Offred's distinction in several ways. Firstly she is being active by lying down because her mind is active. She is thereby asserting her independence in that she has not 'been laid to rest' by a more powerful force. Lay is also American slang for a person to have sex with someone, as in 'a good lay'. Her Handmaid's function is procreation, but when she lies down, she remembers her former identity as an independent educated woman, mother, wife and daughter.

6   Luke to Offred when discussing the dangers of saving plastic bags, Chapter 5. This is the first indication that Offred has a daughter. Her role as a mother is one of Offred's strongest motivations for resisting conformity to Gilead.

7   Offred in reflecting on Serena Joy's past as she passes the Wife on her way into the house, Chapter 8. Offred is aware of the irony that Serena Joy is a victim of precisely what she stood for in the time before. She made televised speeches about the sanctity of the home, and how women should stay at home. These speeches, however, were part of her career. Now, due to the need for women to be protected, she can no longer continue her career. Other than the occasional visit to another Wife, or a Birth Day, she must spend her time at home. It is clear that she is frustrated by the limitations on her life.

8   Offred remembers the time a woman snatched her daughter from the supermarket, Chapter 12. This incident from the time before foreshadowed Offred's daughter being 'snatched' from her and given 'by the Lord' to an older woman to raise.

9   Offred prepares herself for the Ceremony, Chapter 12. Offred is anxious, but must not appear so. In another sense she is being created, in that the Ceremony gives her momentary importance within the household. If she conceives, her identity will be valued within society.

10   One of Aunt Lydia's teachings that Offred recalls during her bath, Chapter 12. Aunt Lydia uses only part of the biblical passage 'Blessed are the meek' to preach the ideal of obedience. The entire passage is 'Blessed are the meek

for they shall inherit the earth.' This is only one of many examples of Aunt Lydia's distortion of biblical authority in order to further the 'Christian' ideals of Gilead.

■ Self-test answers Chapters 13–23

Who? What? Why? When? Where? How?
1 The washroom.
2 For smuggling Handmaids into Canada. They are part of the Mayday resistance movement.
3 Museum guard, midwestern bank president, a vodka ad and shoemaker from an old fairy-tale.
4 Above Offred, towards the head of the bed.
5 A knife.
6 The Quakers.
7 The mid-eighties.
8 Pornography and feminism.
9 Aunt Lydia tells Janine, so that Janine can inform her of accomplices. Janine then spreads the incredible story through the silently whispered Handmaid grapevine.
10 Larynx, valance, quince, zygote, limp and gorge.

Prove it
1 Janine 'seemed almost proud' of her testimonial of being gang raped and having an abortion. Unlike the others, her story is probably true. Janine has also become Aunt Lydia's favoured pupil in Chapter 22 because the Aunt thinks that Janine is a true believer.
2 Offred's shoe softens and her foot becomes warm with increased blood when Nick's foot touches hers. Offred also learns of an underground espionage ring, that has been smuggling Handmaids out of Gilead. This will later emerge as the Mayday resistance movement.
3 When Moira is tortured in Chapter 15, Aunt Lydia justifies the electrocution and physical injury by saying, 'For our purposes your feet and your hands are not essential.' Her choice of words also reinforces this idea in that the Handmaids, for Aunt Lydia, have no purpose of their own.
4 She cries during the prayers, and after the Ceremony she is hostile to Offred.
5 She butters her skin for protection from dryness in the hope that she will still be attractive when she 'gets out'. She also feels guilty about sexually desiring Nick. She thinks of Luke during the embrace with Nick and wonders if he would understand her betrayal.
6 Offred imagines the gossip between the Wives about their Handmaids. They complain and brag about their Handmaids as if they are children.
7 When Offred's mother chastised Offred for taking her freedom for granted, Offred's response was that her mother was getting into an argument over nothing. This attitude shows that she did not appreciate how her mother's generation had suffered from inequality.
8 Moira is able to pass for Aunt Elizabeth because the Angels are not permitted to look at her.
9 When he asks her to kiss him 'as if you meant it', she thinks that he is sad. She realises during her first meeting in his office that he is isolated and lonely

too. She cannot, however, forgive him. She says: 'But if you happen to be a man, sometime in the future, and you've made it this far, please remember: you will never be subjected to the temptation of feeling you must forgive, a man, as a woman.'

10 The Commander's office is full of books. For this reason Guardians, not Marthas, clean it.

What is the significance?

1 Nick's boot touches Offred's foot before the household prayers, Chapter 14. Offred's foot comes alive with the bodily contact. This anticipates the growing attraction between Offred and Nick, and anticipates their embrace in chapter 17.

2 Offred comments on the readings from the Bible during the prayers, Chapter 15. The basis for the Handmaids' surrogate mother function comes from the story of Rachel and Leah in the Bible. Rachel could not have children, so she gave her handmaid to Jacob to bear children for her. See Genesis, 30:1-8.

3 Offred is referring to the Bible, which is kept locked up and to which only the Commander has the key, Chapter 15. No one is allowed to read the Bible except the Commander because if they were, they would see how its authority has been perverted and distorted by the military as a means of control, and a revolt would ensue. Later in the chapter Offred cites distortions of the Beatitudes, but she is unable to prove them.

4 Offred complains about the Commander's official dress during the Ceremony, Chapter 16. This comment foreshadows Offred's and the Commander's attempt at old-fashioned lovemaking.

5 Offred longs for physical and emotional intimacy with Luke after the Ceremony, Chapter 17. This anticipates her relationship with Nick. She will fall in love with Nick, and tell him her real name.

6 Lying in bed she contrasts images of herself now and in the time before, Chapter 18. In the time before she felt protected and her body was alive with her unborn daughter. Now she feels dry and white, hard and granular. The creative force of her body has dried up, not through lack of sex, but through lack of love. This is how Offred views herself, but she hopes that one day she will be loved again. Her hope of future love, especially with Luke, is vital to her survival.

7 Offred's mother justifying her feminist convictions to Luke and Offred, Chapter 20. Ironically her feminist generation contributed to the loss of women's rights in Gilead. She is seen to be blamed, not absolved by history. Is she absolved two centuries later?

8 Offred comparing the films she watches at the Red Centre to the films she watched in her geography lessons at secondary school, Chapter 20. 'Thousands of years before', plays with the sense of time in the novel. To her, Gilead is so different from 'the time before' that her secondary school years seem like another millennium. She is creating distance between Gilead and the time before. In fact, the past and present are not so far apart, which is all the more disturbing for the reader.

9 Offred's summation of the Handmaid's mixed feelings of admiration and insecurity towards Moira's escape from the red Centre, Chapter 22. Moira is loose in many senses of the word. She is on the loose in Gilead. The Handmaids are threatened by the thought that she may be caught at any time, and are disturbed by the possibilities of her punishment. The idea of Moira being set loose from her Handmaid identity is equally unnerving. The Handmaids are losing their will to be independent. Thirdly, Moira is a loose woman in the sexual sense, working at Jezebel's, at the time of Offred's recollection.

10   Offred's delight in playing Scrabble, Chapter 23. Offred thinks that the letter
counters would taste acidic because she is attacking the Commander in a
cryptic way by spelling words that reflect her situation as a 'two-legged
womb', and thereby reminding the Commander of his reproductive failure.
She dares to spell 'limp', which is an explicit assault on the Commander's
sexual prowess. She enjoys special powers afforded by the game, such as the
power to read, write, speak and criticise.

■ Self-test answers Chapters 24–39

Who? What? Why? When? Where? How?

1   She is 33.
2   She has one more chance.
3   They are machines that print out prayers. These prayers can be purchased as
a mark of piety.
4   Islamic fanatics.
5   Labour Day.
6   They were declared Sons of Jacob, a patriarch in the Old Testament. As Sons
of Jacob they were given special status and the choice to return to Israel or
convert.
7   She recognises the club that the Commander takes her to as the hotel she
used to frequent with Luke when he was married.
8   Eight or nine months.
9   She was sent to the Colonies as an Unwoman to clean up toxic waste and
radiation spills.
10   He realises that she is a dangerous person to be associated with, especially
as they were in her apartment without a permit. Luke did not want to give
the authorities any reason to be suspicious of his family, and thereby
jeopardise their hope of escape.

Prove it

1   In Chapter 25, the Commander seems surprised that Offred cannot keep the
hand lotion in her room. He is also perplexed as to why the Handmaids are
kept under close surveillance.
2   Offred asks the Commander the meaning of the message in her closet. When
he explains that the phrase is a pseudo-Latin schoolboy prank, she realises
that the previous Offred must have learned the phrase from the Commander.
She also learns that her predecessor hung herself after Serena Joy found out
about her unofficial relationship with the Commander.
3   The Commander quotes Napoleon in his justification for women being worse
off in Gilead, Chapter 32. 'You can't make an omelette without breaking
eggs.' Napoleon made the original statement in justification of the deaths he
caused in building his empire. The Commander's use of the saying exposes
the ruthlessness underlying his gentle exterior.
4   If a Handmaid has a miscarriage, or if her baby is declared an Unbaby, she
holds the same status as a Handmaid who has never conceived. If, after three
postings, she does not produce a healthy baby, she will be declared an
Unwoman and sent to the Colonies.
5   The privileged Daughters of the Commanders have to take vows of silence
and subservience to their husbands during the Prayvaganza wedding
ceremonies.

6   Offred often wonders whether Nick approves or disapproves of her relationship with the Commander. In Chapter 28 she wonders 'How does he feel, pimping in this ambiguous way for the Commander? Does it fill him with disgust, or make him want more of me, want me more?' In Chapter 36, as Nick drives her and the Commander to Jezebel's, she tries to read his body language: 'His posture disapproves of me, or am I imagining it?' As she gets out of the car she notices Nick looking at her and wonders, 'Is it contempt I read, or indifference, is this merely what he expected of me?'

7   The existence of the club is proof that woman are still debased and regarded as sex objects in Gilead. Offred, herself, notices only their bodies in her descriptions of the other women at the club.

8   She tells Offred that after her capture she was not taken back to the Red Centre. She was taken elsewhere, which she cannot bring herself to talk about. Her last comment, 'All I can say is they didn't leave any marks', hints that she suffered a water torture.

9   Offred cannot forgive the Commander for being a member of a regime that knowingly and willingly subjected her mother to a life of slavery, drudgery and ultimately painful death. During his attempt to have old-fashioned intercourse with her, she tries to convince herself that he is not a monster, but the whole narrative reveals that she finds him repulsive.

10 There are many instances in this section where she cannot clearly recall information. In Chapter 39, for instance, she is confused in her allusion to Cinderella: 'I must be back at the house before midnight; otherwise I'll turn into a pumpkin, or was that the coach?'

What is the significance?

1   Offred ponders her intensified, albeit mixed, feelings towards Serena Joy, Chapter 26. Although Offred enjoys sexual and emotional victories over Serena Joy, she is jealous of the Wife's status and power. If Serena Joy knew of Offred's liaisons with the Commander, the Handmaid would ultimately be subject to the older woman's power. Offred knows that she is the woman with more to lose.

2   Offred informs the reader of the five types of prayers one can purchase in Gilead as she walks by Soul Scrolls with Ofglen, Chapter 27. These prayers indicate Gileadean values. Notice that there are prayers for wealth, but no prayers for charity.

3   Offred thinks of the Book of Job when she thinks of the various associations of the word job, Chapter 28. The Book of Job comes from the Old Testament. It tells the story of a wealthy farmer, Job, whose faith is tested through loss of everything he valued, such as his family and his livelihood. The biblical story is significant in that it parallels Offred's situation. In the Book of Job, Job never doubts his faith, and as a result God rewards him by restoring everything he had lost. In this chapter we learn of the transition from democratic America to the creation of the Republic of Gilead. Offred loses her job and her sense of independence. She has also lost her family and her individual freedom. The obvious similarity to the story of Job makes us wonder if, like Job, her former life will be restored to her, or if she will continue to suffer because, unlike Job, she has lost her faith. Think of all the instances of Offred's lack of faith.

4   Offred confuses this reference from King Lear when realising that she is falling in love with Nick, Chapter 30. The line from King Lear is 'Ripeness is all'. Both references pertain to betrayal – his eldest daughter's and his own vanity betrayed King Lear. Offred feels that the context in which she is falling in love with Nick does not justify her betrayal of Luke.

5   Offred recalls the routine Handmaid prayers at the Red Centre, Chapter 30. This is a reversal of a traditional Jewish prayer in which men offer thanks that they are not women. It is one of many routine prayers of abasement and obedience that the Handmaids had to repeat at the Red Centre. The significance of these prayers is their contrast to Offred's version of the Lord's Prayer which follows. Offred's prayer is about hope, forgiveness, charity and spiritual salvation.

6   Offred remembers some graffiti on the cubicle at the Red Centre, during the Prayvaganza, Chapter 37. Offred has this memory following the marriage vows where the Daughters pledge subservience and silence to their husbands. Offred resists indoctrination by ridiculing the powerful authoritarian figures in Gilead.

7   Offred asks the Commander who the people are at the club, Chapter 36. The significance of this question lies in the contrast between Offred's and the Commander's perspectives. Offred was referring to the women. Women are now more interesting to Offred in her female dominated existence. The Commander naturally assumes that she is referring to the men. His response demonstrates his sexist perspective, and she has to ask specifically who the women are.

8   Moira to Offred about Offred's Commander, at Jezebel's, Chapter 38. Moira suggests that Offred's Commander has only brought her on this 'night out' as a power trip. Moira sees the Commander for what he is, as opposed to Offred who likes to give him the benefit of the doubt. After hearing Moira's story, however, Offred feels differently about him.

9   Offred's reaction to Moira's resignation towards her life at Jezebel's, Chapter 38. Offred is disappointed and threatened to discover Moira has lost her fighting spirit and accepted her life as a prostitute. Moira's courage and strength have been a talisman to Offred's will to survive. If Moira has been defeated, what chance is there for the less brave, such as Offred?

10   Moira to Offred about the latter's mother, Chapter 39. Offred is ignorant of the reality of life in the Colonies, as she has not seen the same films as Moira. Death from radiation poisoning is a cruelly painful way to die. The workers in the Colonies are merely cheap and dispensable labour. Moira points out that Offred should not feel relieved that her mother is still alive if she is living in the Colonies.

■ Self-test answers
Chapters 40–Historical Notes

Who? What? Why? When? Where? How?

1   Above the garage.
2   High summer.
3   The day before it took place.
4   The university.
5   Biblical authority: Deuteronomy 22:23–29, 'If a man find a betrothed damsel in the field, and the man force her, and lie with her: then the man only that lay with her shall die.'
6   To see if the old Ofglen is hanging on the Wall.

7   She finds telltale lipstick on her cloak, and the purple sequinned outfit.
8   Serena Joy.
9   Bangor, Maine, a prominent way station on the Underground Femaleroad.
10   University of Denay, Nunavit, June 25, 2195.

Prove it

1   In Chapter 40 she is cagey about what really happened. Obviously the memory is so special she wishes to keep it private. The privacy of their relationship is reinforced in the following chapter when she shares her real name with Nick, but not with the audience.

2   In Chapter 41 she tells him her real name.

3   Offred's fantasy was of Luke rescuing her. By Chapter 41 she no longer wants to escape because she has fallen in love with Nick. It is no longer Luke's memory that gives her the will to survive, but Nick's love.

4   Offred makes all the right motions: 'I've leaned forward to touch the rope in front of me, in time with the others, both hands on it, the rope hairy, sticky with tar in the hot sun, then placed my hand on my heart to show my unity with the Salvagers and my consent, and my complicity in the death of this woman.' Nonetheless, when the executioners drag the rope to lift the woman off the scaffold, she looks at the grass instead of the woman's jerking death, and describes the rope. Offred cannot bear to watch the spectacle because she knows unconsciously that it could easily be her up there. It is worse not knowing what the Handmaids' crimes are, because our imaginations can run wild with reasons, such as one of the Handmaids being caught having a sexual relationship with a Guardian.

5   At the Particicution Ofglen breaks through the crowd and kicks the man convicted of rape unconscious before the others get to him. Even such an act of mercy requires courage.

6   When Offred gives her the password, her carefully worded response indicates that while she is aware of the movement and the password, she is not a part of it. She warns Offred, moreover, of her involvement in such a scheme: ' "That isn't a term I remember. I'm surprised you do. You ought to make an effort ..." She pauses. "To clear your mind of such ..." She pauses again. "Echoes." '

7   When she realises that Ofglen took her own life, rather than betray the resistance movement, Offred is relieved. She feels that she has escaped danger this time, but she is too frightened of the consequences to risk resistance again. She vows that she will 'accept my lot' because the events of the day have made her aware of the full extent of the regime's power.

8   As the black van pulls up to the house, Offred realises that there were always weapons around, such as the garden shears, kitchen knives or Serena's knitting needles, that she could have used to take her life, if she had really wanted to.

9   Frederick R. Waterford shares more similarities to Offred's Commander than B. Frederick Judd does. In addition to the obvious similarities outlined at the symposium, this man's interest in female fashion, as evident in his designing of the Handmaids' attire, would account for his collection of women's fashion magazines that he lets Offred read.

10   Faithful to anthropological research, anthropologists study other cultures objectively without passing judgement on the morality or any other aspect of the culture being researched. As he cannot identify either Offred or her Commander with certainty, the value of Offred's document as an artefact of the early Gileadean period is dismissed.

What is the significance?

1 Offred remembering that even during her first time with Nick, she knew she would be leaving, Chapter 40. The fact that this comment is made in retrospect prepares us for the fact that the relationship will be intense, but short-lived. This in turn heightens the tension throughout the remaining chapters.

2 Offred to the audience, Chapter 41. This statement is a reworking of French philosopher René Descartes' 'I think, therefore I am'. Her narrative is validated by the idea of communication.

3 Offred is pleased that Ofglen is giving up on trying to get her help in the resistance movement, Chapter 41. In this chapter Offred is in love with Nick. Love has transformed her life so significantly that she no longer wishes to be rescued, or to escape. Like most people in the 'honeymoon' phase of a relationship, Offred has become self absorbed. Ofglen's information about the regime and the resistance movement, which used to be of such interest to Offred, is now irritating. Offred temporarily adjusts to life in Gilead: 'I have made a life for myself, here, of a sort. That must have been what the settlers' wives thought, and women who survived wars, if they still had a man.' Momentarily, Offred is also forgetting the danger she faces.

4 The bell is tolling to call women to the Women's Salvaging, Chapter 42. Tolling bells traditionally signify death. In this context the bells are tolling to call women to a public execution. Symbolically, however, the bells could also be warning of Ofglen's imminent death and Offred's sudden departure from the life she's grown to love.

5 Offred's reaction to Ofglen's news that the man was a member of the resistance movement, posing as a Guardian, Chapter 43. This foreshadows the revelation that Nick is a member of the Mayday resistance movement.

6 Offred comments on returning to her routines after the morning's Women's Salvaging and Particicution, Chapter 44. This is an ironic statement as events are about to get dramatically worse. The use of irony is a narrative device used to create the element of surprise.

7 Offred comments on the cessation of Nick's whistling following the confrontation with Serena Joy, Chapter 45. Overhearing Serena's Joy's disclosure, Nick has probably left to contact the resistance movement to rescue Offred.

8 Offred's thought as she is being helped into the black van, Chapter 46. This sentiment recalls the closing of Tennessee Williams' play *A Streetcar Named Desire*. As a result of her nervous breakdown, Blanche Dubois is led away by two men from a mental hospital. She goes willingly and declares, 'I have always relied on the kindness of strangers.' Blanche's meaning is that strangers have always been kinder to her than her own family. Like Blanche, Offred is being escorted away from an explosive situation, but whether she is going to a worse existence is beyond her control.

9 The name of the university hosting the symposium on Gileadean Studies, in the Historical Notes. Atwood took the name from the Dene people of Canada's Northwest territories. The Dene are about to become the first self-governing group of North American native peoples in an area called Nunavut. The name also sounds like 'Deny none of it', which directs us to believe Offred's story as the truth.

10 An achievement of Frederick R. Waterford, one of the two possible identities of Offred's Commander, in the Historical Notes. If this Frederick were Offred's Commander, his enjoyment of word play would account for his desire to play Scrabble. The play on words to create the label for such a Barbaric practice also casts the innocent Scrabble games in a more sinister light.

Notes

Notes